COOKING
WITH SHEREEN

Rockstar
Dinners!

Because You're Fancy!

SHEREEN PAVLIDES

PAGE STREET
PUBLISHING CO.

PAGE STREET
PUBLISHING CO.

First published in 2023 by
Page Street Publishing Co.
27 Congress Street, Suite 1511
Salem, MA 01970
www.pagestreetpublishing.com

Distributed by Macmillan, sales in Canada by The Canadian Manda Group.

27   26   25   24   23   2   3   4   5

ISBN-13: 978-1-64567-990-5
ISBN-10: 1-64567-990-X

Library of Congress Control Number: 2022946835

Cover and book design by Meg Baskis for Page Street Publishing Co.
Photography by Ken Goodman, author image on page 173 by Sue McDaid

Printed and bound in the United States

TO MY HUSBAND, ANDREAS

You love to eat; I love to cook. We're a perfect match.
You're my soul mate through food, love and life.
I'm grateful for your support as I painstakingly
pursued my dreams; you always
believed in me. We've just begun.

TO OUR CHILDREN, COSTAS AND ISABELLA

Pursue your passion, never give up, no dream is
ever too big, you're both capable as long as you're
willing to keep pushing and do the work, the
process will pave the way and when you get there
be prepared for the real work to begin.
As yiayiá would always say, "Make your passion your job
and you'll never work a day in your life."

IN LOVING MEMORY OF MY MOTHER.

Rest in Peace.
February 20, 1946 to August 8, 2022

TABLE *of* CONTENTS

INTRODUCTION

Be selfish! You're allowed. This book is for you. Your family and friends will reap the rewards but first begin by allowing yourself to enjoy the process of making homemade food. It should never feel like a chore. You're composing edible art that your loved ones will praise you for, making you feel happy, empowered and gain confidence through cooking. It feels so freakin' good! And tastes even better!

When I develop a recipe, it starts with inspiration, research of the dish (even if I know it) and as I cook, my senses take over through taste, smells, visuals, aha moments and experiences that twist the concept from my initial plan. That's what cooking great food is all about to me. One's expression. Traditional sets boundaries; it's boring! Plus it's been done a thousand times over. My passion and creativity do not create like that, so I won't and I don't. I create everything with you in my heart and mind to please through taste.

I aim to construct a dish that blows you away, makes you moan, even groan! That's my goal . . . and I want you to feel amazing while making it and eating it. I've always been infatuated with all cultures and cuisines. It's the bold, exotic and unique flavors that keep me alive. I can't pick just one cuisine, so we'll make a little of everything, from Asian to Mexican, Italian, Greek, French, Mediterranean and more infused with inventiveness and excitement for all occasions: holidays, weekends and for everyday, making you feel like a rockstar chef in your own kitchen.

There are no rules in cooking; cook with passion, be creative!

CHEFIE TIP

I use Diamond Crystal kosher salt for all of my recipes. If you're using a different brand, please adjust the measurements to taste.

IT'S ITALIAN

From Scratch. Some Italian. Some Italian American . . . Relax!

GARGANELLI ALL'ARRABBIATA

Garganelli is an egg-based pasta similar to penne, and it sucks this delicious spicy sauce into its tubular shape for the perfect bite. I strongly recommend making it fresh, it's insane! Actually life-changing but certainly, you can substitute for ¾ pound (340 g) dried penne or rigatoni and cook according to the package directions. I have this thing with canned tomato puree; I don't care for it. It tastes metallic to me. So when using San Marzano tomatoes, don't use the canned tomato puree. If you like, save for other uses.

SERVES 6

2 (28-ounce [794-g]) jars fresh canned tomatoes (page 140) or cans whole peeled San Marzano tomatoes

⅓ cup (80 ml) olive oil

6 large garlic cloves - minced

10 to 12 Calabrian chile peppers packed in oil - stemmed and minced (2 to 3 tablespoons [16 to 29 g])

kosher salt

fresh finely ground black pepper

½ cup (12 g) fresh packed basil leaves + 3 tablespoons (9 g) fresh basil - sliced, to garnish

1 pound (454 g) homemade garganelli (page 153)

3 tablespoons (45 ml) extra virgin olive oil

3 tablespoons (11 g) chopped fresh Italian parsley

CHEFIE TIP

Eliminate the chiles and you have a classic marinara (makes about 32 ounces [946 ml]) for pizza (page 150), pasta or Eggplant Rollatini (page 21)

In a medium bowl, crush the tomatoes with clean hands. If using San Marzanos, drain the tomatoes, place them into a medium bowl, and crush them with clean hands. Don't be a wimp! Fill the cans one-quarter of the way with cold water, and swirl to release the tomato juice from the walls of the cans. Add the tomato water to the bowl with the tomatoes.

In a 12-inch (30.5-cm) sauté pan, heat ⅓ cup (80 ml) olive oil over medium heat. When the oil shimmers, about 30 seconds, add the garlic and chiles. Reduce the heat to medium-low, and sauté until you can smell the *gálick*, 1 to 2 minutes. Add the crushed tomatoes to the pan. Season with 2 teaspoons (12 g) kosher salt and ½ teaspoon pepper. Add ½ cup (12 g) of the basil and bring to a full bubble over medium-high heat. Reduce to simmer and cook, about 25 minutes until the liquid is reduced, stirring occasionally.

Using a handheld immersion blender, puree the tomatoes in the pan until the sauce is chunky smooth. Taste the sauce and season with additional salt and pepper to your liking.

Meanwhile, bring a 6-quart (5.5-L) pot of salted water to a rolling bubble. Add the homemade garganelli to the boiling water and stir. Briefly cover the pot to quickly return the water to a bubble. Then uncover once it's bubbling. Don't let it bubble over. Cook uncovered until tender, 2 minutes. Strain, reserving ½ cup (120 ml) of the pasta liquid, just in case you need it to thin the sauce. Stir the pasta directly into the sauce and simmer, about 2 minutes to marry the two together.

Remove the pan from the heat. Add the 3 tablespoons (45 ml) extra virgin olive oil and parsley, because you're fancy. Stir and transfer to a large family-sized pasta bowl. Garnish with the sliced basil because you're extra fancy.

SHORT RIB RAGÙ LASAGNA FROM SCRATCH

This recipe takes time, so plan ahead for a Sunday or make it for Christmas like I do. It's comforting and absolutely delicious.

SERVES 10 TO 12

2 pounds (907 g) bone-in short ribs (4 to 5) - excess fat trimmed

kosher salt

fresh finely ground black pepper

2 tablespoons (30 ml) olive oil

3 (28-ounce [794-g]) jars fresh canned tomatoes (page 140) or 1 (28-ounce [794-g]) can whole peeled San Marzano tomatoes and 1 (28-ounce [794-g]) can crushed tomatoes

1 medium yellow onion - finely diced (about 1 cup [160 g])

5 to 7 garlic cloves - minced

½ cup (120 ml) chardonnay

1½ teaspoons (1.5 g) dried oregano

1½ teaspoons (1.5 g) dried parsley

Heat the oven to 350°F (177°C). Dry the short ribs really well with heavy-duty paper towels and season both sides with 1¾ teaspoon (10.5 g) salt and ½ teaspoon pepper.

In a 5½-quart (5-L) Dutch oven, heat the oil over medium heat. When the oil shimmers, add the short ribs. Sear until they are nicely browned and caramelized, 2 to 3 minutes, on three to four sides. Transfer to a plate and set aside. Carefully degrease the pot, leaving ¼ cup (60 ml) of the oil.

In a medium bowl, crush the tomatoes with clean hands. If using San Marzanos, drain the tomatoes, place them in a medium bowl, and crush them with clean hands. Add the crushed tomatoes to the same bowl. Fill the cans one-third of the way with cold water and swirl to release the tomato juice from the walls of cans. Add the tomato water to the bowl with the tomatoes.

Add the onions to the Dutch oven and season with ½ teaspoon salt and ⅛ teaspoon pepper. Sauté until tender, 2 to 3 minutes. Add the garlic and sauté until fragrant, about 30 seconds.

Deglaze with wine and cook until it's reduced by half, about 1 minute.

Add the tomatoes, dried oregano and dried parsley to the pot. Season with 2 teaspoons (12 g) salt and ¾ teaspoon pepper. Stir. Return the short ribs to the pot, nestling them under the sauce. Increase the heat to medium-high and bring the sauce to a gentle bubble. Cut the heat and cover the pot.

Place the pot in the oven and cook until the short ribs are uber tender, falling off the bones, 2 hours to 2 hours 15 minutes. Remove the pot from the oven and shred the meat into the sauce, discarding the bones (or keep the bones in a freezer-safe container and store them in the freezer to use for making Homemade Beef Stock, page 170).

(continued)

SHORT RIB RAGÙ LASAGNA FROM SCRATCH

(continued)

1 large egg

3 pounds (1.4 kg) whole-milk ricotta cheese

⅓ cup (33 g) grated Parmigiano-Reggiano + more to taste

¼ cup (15 g) chopped fresh Italian parsley

½ teaspoon freshly grated nutmeg

1 pound (454 g) homemade lasagna sheets (page 153)

12 ounces (336 g) part-skim mozzarella cheese - grated on large hole of box grater (3 cups)

fresh oregano leaves - to garnish

CHEFIE TIPS

You'll need parchment paper, two pairs of tongs, kitchen rubber gloves and lots of clean kitchen towels to help you through with ease while boiling the noodles, so you don't burn your hands.

While making the fresh lasagna sheets, keep the rolled out sheets lined between parchment paper or clean kitchen towels, not touching. You can do this step 1 to 2 days ahead and refrigerate.

Taste the sauce and season to taste with salt and pepper, if needed.

Meanwhile, in an extra-large bowl, whisk the egg. Add the ricotta, Parmigiano-Reggiano, parsley, nutmeg, 1 teaspoon salt and ¼ teaspoon pepper and stir until combined. Cover and refrigerate; remove the cheese mixture from the refrigerator 30 minutes before assembling the lasagna.

Make the lasagna noodles (page 153). The recipe will make 8 (12 x 6–inch [30.5 x 15–cm]) sheets of lasagna. Spread 2 to 3 (½-cup [120-ml]) ladles of sauce into the bottom of a 9 x 12 x 2½–inch (23 x 30.5 x 6–cm) baking dish.

Bring a 6-quart (5.5-L) pot of salted water to a rolling bubble. Use several ladles of this water to thin the ragù, as needed.

Boil the lasagna noodles, 2 sheets at a time, making sure they don't stick together, until par-cooked, 30 seconds. Use two pairs of tongs to remove each sheet, grabbing one at each end, dripping off the excess water. Place the noodles on a sheet of parchment paper until cool enough to handle. You can use kitchen gloves to protect your hands from the hot noodles as you work.

Evenly divide the ingredients, working in four layers: Place 2 noodles into the baking dish side by side over the sauce. Spread the ricotta mixture with an offset spatula to evenly coat the noodles. Spread 2 (½-cup [120-ml]) ladles of the sauce on top. Repeat layering the noodles with the ricotta mixture and the sauce. Lightly sprinkle with Parmigiano-Reggiano and evenly sprinkle the mozzarella cheese on top. Cover with foil and place the dish on a rimmed baking sheet.

Bake until cooked through, 40 to 45 minutes. Remove the foil and increase the heat to 400°F (204°C). Continue baking until melty and lightly golden, about 15 minutes.

Remove the lasagna from the oven and let it rest, 20 to 25 minutes to set; otherwise it'll fall apart if you rip into it right away. Garnish with fresh oregano, because you're fancy. Cut into squares. Serve any remaining short rib ragù on the side.

LOBSTER FRA DIAVOLO FETTUCCINE

This is my father's favorite dish. When I make it, I always think of him. Fra diavolo and arrabbiata (page 10) are very similar, both have a fiery kick. The difference is, fra diavolo is an Italian American invention mostly served with lobster or seafood, and arrabbiata is a traditional Italian dish served with pasta, vegetarian-style.

SERVES 6

4 (6-ounce [170-g]) lobster tails - split down the back, digestive tract removed

½ teaspoon cayenne pepper

kosher salt

fresh finely ground black pepper

4 tablespoons (56 g) unsalted butter

2 (28-ounce [794-g]) jars fresh canned tomatoes (page 140) or 2 cans whole peeled San Marzano tomatoes

3 tablespoons (45 ml) olive oil

6 garlic cloves - minced

5 to 6 Calabrian chiles packed in oil - stemmed, finely chopped

¾ to 1 teaspoon pepperoncino (red pepper flakes)

½ cup (120 ml) chardonnay

Leave the lobster in the shells and season the meat with cayenne, ½ teaspoon salt and ¼ teaspoon pepper.

In a 12-inch (30.5-cm) sauté pan over medium-low heat, melt the butter. Place the lobster in the pan, meat side down. Reduce the heat to low and cover the pan to slowly poach the lobster in the butter until just cooked through, 5 to 7 minutes. Flip the lobster tails halfway through poaching and baste the lobster with the *buttah*. Don't overcook 'em or they'll be tough. Transfer to a plate, reserving the butter in the pan.

Meanwhile: In a medium bowl, finely crush the tomatoes with clean hands. If using San Marzanos, drain the tomatoes, place them in a medium bowl, and finely crush them with clean hands. Don't be a wimp! Save the tomato puree for another use if desired. Fill the cans one-quarter of the way with cold water and swirl to release the tomato juices from the walls of the cans. Add the tomato water to the bowl with the tomatoes.

In the same sauté pan, add the oil to the butter, and heat over medium heat. Add the garlic, chiles and pepperoncino and sauté until you can smell the *gálick*, about 30 seconds. Deglaze with wine and cook until reduced by half, 2 to 3 minutes.

(continued)

LOBSTER FRA DIAVOLO FETTUCCINE *(continued)*

½ cup (12 g) packed fresh basil leaves

1 pound (454 g) homemade fettuccine (page 153)

¼ cup (15 g) chopped fresh Italian parsley

Add the crushed tomatoes and basil, and season with 2 teaspoons (12 g) kosher salt and ½ teaspoon pepper. Remove the lobster meat from the shells and pull the lobster meat apart into bite-sized pieces. Keep the lobster warm and toss the shells in with the sauce. This will create a lobster stock–like *flavah*. Bring the sauce to a bubble over medium-high heat, then reduce to simmer.

Cook about 25 minutes until the sauce reduces slightly and the flavors build, stirring periodically.

Remove and discard the shells from the sauce. Taste the sauce and season to your liking with salt and pepper, if needed.

Meanwhile, bring a 6-quart (5.5-L) pot of salted water to a rolling bubble.

Add the homemade fettuccine to the boiling water and stir. Cook uncovered until the pasta is tender, about 2 minutes. Strain, reserving ½ cup (120 ml) of the pasta liquid, just in case you need it to thin the sauce. Stir the pasta directly into the sauce and simmer, 1 to 2 minutes to marry the two together.

Briefly cover the pot to quickly return the water to a bubble. Then uncover once it's bubbling. Don't let it bubble over.

Remove the pan from the heat. Stir in the lobster until warmed through. Evenly sprinkle parsley over the top because you're fancy. Toss and transfer to a large family-sized pasta bowl.

PAPPARDELLE BOLOGNESE

I know what you're thinking: Milk? Yep. It's an old-school traditional style of making Bolognese in Bologna. It gives a creamy texture and makes the color of the Bolognese pretty. I don't like red wine in my sauce, it's too tannic and heavy. White wine makes it lighter and fruity and I also opt for chicken stock, again for a lighter flavor. I'm not big on a thick and heavy sauce; my Italian mother-in-law, Esther, loved that about my cooking.

SERVES 6

¾ pound (340 g) trimmed beef chuck - cubed

¾ pound (340 g) trimmed pork butt - cubed

4 ounces (113 g) diced pancetta

½ cup (65 g) peeled, minced carrots

½ cup (80 g) minced yellow onion

½ cup (50 g) minced celery

fresh finely ground black pepper

2 tablespoons (28 g) unsalted butter

kosher salt

¼ cup (60 ml) tomato paste

1 cup (240 ml) chardonnay

3 cups (720 ml) Homemade Chicken Stock (page 169)

1 cup (242 g) fresh jar canned tomatoes (page 140) or whole peeled San Marzano tomatoes - drained and crushed by hand

1 cup (240 ml) whole milk

Heat the oven to 325°F (163°C).

In a food processor fitted with the blade attachment, add the cubed meat and pulse until finely ground. Alternatively, you can use a meat grinder or a cleaver.

Heat a 5½-quart (5-L) Dutch oven over medium heat. Add the pancetta and cook, rendering the fat, about 2 minutes. Add the carrots, onions and celery, and season with ¼ teaspoon pepper. (It has enough salt from the pancetta.)

Toss in the *buttah* and melt. Sauté the vegetables until tender, 4 to 5 minutes. Transfer the pancetta and vegetables to a medium bowl; this allows the meat to brown rather than steam because the pot will be too crowded.

Add the ground meat to the pot. Season with 1¼ teaspoons (7.5 g) salt and ½ teaspoon pepper. Sauté until browned, 5 to 6 minutes.

Add the tomato paste and cook, about 2 minutes to caramelize, deepening the flavor.

Deglaze with wine and cook until reduced by half, about 1 minute. Add the chicken stock and tomatoes, and bring to a gentle simmer. Return the pancetta and vegetables to the pot. Pour in the milk and stir. Cut the heat and cover. The sauce will be thin, *donta* you worry. Place the pot in the oven and braise until the meat is uber tender and reduced by two-thirds, about 2 hours.

(continued)

PAPPARDELLE BOLOGNESE *(continued)*

1 cup (100 g) loosely packed freshly grated Parmigiano-Reggiano + more to garnish

1 pound (454 g) fresh pappardelle (page 153)

Remove the Bolognese from the oven and stir in 1 cup (100 g) Parmigiano-Reggiano.

Bring a 6-quart (5.5-L) pot of salted water to a rolling bubble. Add the pappardelle and stir. Briefly cover the pot to quickly return the water to a bubble. Then uncover once it's bubbling. Don't let it bubble over. Cook uncovered until the pasta is tender but still a little chewy, 2 to 3 minutes.

Using a spider, fine-mesh strainer or tongs, drain the pasta, reserving 1 to 2 cups (240 to 480 ml) pasta water. Immediately transfer the pasta to the sauce. Return the pot to the stove over low heat and simmer, 1 to 2 minutes, marrying the two, stirring constantly. Working a little at a time, ladle some pasta water into the Bolognese as needed to thin the sauce.

Divide the pasta among six bowls. Garnish with more freshly grated Parmigiano-Reggiano.

EGGPLANT ROLLATINI

This is my brother-in-law, Nikos', favorite. It's a satisfying, meaty and incredibly flavorful vegetarian dish. Instead of bagged shredded mozzarella, buy the block in the dairy section and grate it yourself; it's creamier. Don't use fresh mozzarella here; shortly after it melts, it firms up with a rubbery texture, and it's best in cold preparations. Check your cheese section at your grocery store for a fresh ricotta or BelGioioso brand ricotta; it's also creamy and delicious.

SERVES 6 TO 8

FOR THE EGGPLANT

3 large globe eggplants (3 pounds [1.4 kg] total)

kosher salt

fresh finely ground black pepper

1¼ cups (156 g) all-purpose flour

1½ to 2 cups (360 to 480 ml) olive oil - divided, as needed

FOR THE RICOTTA MIXTURE

1 large egg

2 cups (490 g) whole-milk ricotta cheese

1 (16-ounce [448-g]) block whole-milk mozzarella - grated on large hole of box grater (4 cups) - divided

¼ cup (25 g) grated Parmigiano-Reggiano

¼ cup (15 g) chopped fresh Italian parsley

4 cups (960 ml) homemade marinara - warmed (see Chefie Tip page 10)

fresh basil - sliced, to garnish

Heat the oven to 375°F (190°C).

TO MAKE THE EGGPLANT: Stem and trim the bottoms of the eggplant. Slice the eggplant lengthwise into ¼-inch- (6 mm-) thick slices. You'll have about 20 slices. Place the eggplant on a wire cooling rack over a baking sheet. Lightly sprinkle salt over the surface of the eggplant on both sides. Let it set, 15 minutes. (This will pull out the excess moisture and bitterness.)

MEANWHILE, MAKE THE RICOTTA MIXTURE: In a medium bowl, whisk the egg. Add the ricotta, 1 cup (112 g) of the mozzarella, Parmigiano-Reggiano, parsley, ½ teaspoon salt and ⅛ teaspoon pepper, and stir until combined.

In a wide, shallow bowl, whisk the flour, 1 teaspoon salt and ¼ teaspoon pepper. Set aside.

Using heavy-duty paper towels, thoroughly wipe the excess salt and moisture from the eggplant until dry. Dredge each eggplant slice in the flour, shaking off the excess, leaving a thin coat of flour over the eggplant.

Heat a 12-inch (30.5-cm) frying pan over medium heat. Add ½ cup (120 ml) olive oil. When the oil shimmers, working in batches, add 3 eggplant slices to the pan at a time. Pan-fry until the eggplant is lightly golden and tender, 2 minutes on each side. Transfer to a paper towel–lined baking sheet. Lightly sprinkle the eggplant with salt.

(continued)

EGGPLANT ROLLATINI *(continued)*

Repeat with the remaining eggplant, adding 2 to 4 tablespoons (30 to 60 ml) olive oil as needed for each batch. (Note: Heat the new oil for 20 seconds before adding the next batch of eggplant.) Halfway through frying, as the flour in the bottom of the pan starts to accumulate too much and begins to burn, carefully remove the oil to a heat-safe bowl, wipe out the skillet, and add ½ cup (120 ml) new olive oil into the skillet.

Divide and ladle 2 cups (480 ml) marinara in the bottom of two 9 x 12–inch (23 x 30.5–cm) baking dishes.

Evenly spread about 2 tablespoons (30 ml) of the ricotta mixture over one side of the eggplant. Starting at the smaller end, gently roll the eggplant into pinwheels (not too tight), and place them seam side down in the baking dish over the sauce. Each baking dish fits about 10 eggplant pinwheels. Divide and ladle the remaining 2 cups (480 ml) marinara over the top of the eggplant among both baking dishes.

Divide and sprinkle remaining 3 cups (336 g) mozzarella cheese over the eggplant among both baking dishes.

Bake, uncovered, until hot, bubbly and the cheese is melted, about 25 minutes. Remove the baking dishes from the oven and let the rollatini rest, 10 minutes. Garnish with basil before serving, because you're fancy.

LEMONY SCAMPI

Scampi means shrimp (prawns). Or use langoustines, as they do in Italy. Skip the pasta and serve the shrimp with my Peasant Bread (page 149) for dipping into the sauce. It's bright, lemony and savory.

SERVES 6

2 pounds (907 g) extra-large wild shrimp (U/21 to U/25) - peeled, deveined, tails on

½ cup (120 ml) olive oil

6 garlic cloves - finely minced

1 lemon - rind peeled into strips with vegetable peeler

kosher salt

fresh finely ground black pepper

½ to ¾ teaspoon pepperoncino (red pepper flakes)

⅓ cup (80 ml) chardonnay or chenin blanc

3 tablespoons (45 ml) freshly squeezed lemon juice

4 tablespoons (196 g) cold unsalted butter - cut into pats

2 tablespoons (7 g) finely chopped fresh Italian parsley

1 tablespoon (2 g) thinly sliced fresh chives

CHEFIE TIP

Don't break the sauce means if you stop stirring the cold butter and crank the heat, the fat and milk solids will break and separate the emulsification, making the sauce oily instead of velvety.

In a large bowl, add the shrimp, olive oil, garlic and lemon peel, and toss to evenly combine. Cover and marinate, 2 to 4 hours in the refrigerator. Remove 30 minutes before cooking.

Season the shrimp with 1¼ teaspoons (7.5 g) salt and ½ teaspoon black pepper.

In a 12-inch (30.5-cm) sauté pan over medium heat, add the shrimp and marinade using a rubber spatula to get all of it out of the bowl and cook until you hear it sizzle, about 1 minute. Reduce the heat to medium-low. Sprinkle in desired amount of pepperoncino and cook until the shrimp are par-cooked and turn slightly pink, about 5 minutes, tossing periodically. Transfer the shrimp with a slotted spoon to a large bowl. The shrimp will only be cooked three-quarters of the way at this point, *donta* you worry.

Increase the heat to medium and deglaze the pan with the wine and lemon juice. Cook until reduced by half, 1 to 1½ minutes. Season with a pinch of salt.

Reduce the heat to low and return the shrimp to the pan. Add the *buttah* and stir until the butter is melted, 1 to 2 minutes. Don't break the sauce (see Chefie Tip)! Remove the pan from the heat and transfer the shrimp and sauce to a medium rimmed platter.

Garnish with parsley and chives, because you're fancy. Serve immediately with fresh, lightly toasted, sliced Peasant Bread (page 149) on the side for dipping.

CLASSIC CHICKEN PICCATA

I like serving this with my Peasant Bread (page 149) to sop up the delicious sauce, as well as a simple salad and a nice, crisp glass of chardonnay or your favorite white wine.

SERVES 3 TO 4

1½ pounds (680 g) boneless, skinless chicken breasts (3 to 4), preferably organic

kosher salt

fresh finely ground black pepper

⅓ cup (41 g) all-purpose flour

1 teaspoon granulated garlic

4 tablespoons (60 ml) olive oil - divided + more as needed

1 large shallot - minced

½ cup (120 ml) Homemade Chicken Stock (page 169)

1 lemon rind - peeled into strips with vegetable peeler

¼ cup (60 ml) freshly squeezed lemon juice

½ lemon - thinly sliced

1½ tablespoons (15 g) capers - drained and rinsed

6 tablespoons (84 g) cold unsalted butter

2 tablespoons (4 g) chopped fresh Italian parsley

CHEFIE TIP

Roll the lemon before squeezing, it loosens the juice.

Place the chicken into a large zipper bag, pushing out the air. Zip the bag and pound the chicken until they're all evenly ½ inch (1 cm) thick. Remove the chicken from the bag and dry it well with heavy-duty paper towels. Season with 1¼ teaspoons (7.5 g) salt and ½ teaspoon pepper on both sides.

In a large, shallow bowl, add the flour, garlic, ¼ teaspoon salt and ⅛ teaspoon pepper and whisk until combined. Dredge the chicken in the flour, shaking off the excess.

Heat a 12-inch (30.5-cm) frying pan over medium heat for 1 minute. Add 3 tablespoons (45 ml) olive oil. When the oil shimmers, add the chicken to the pan. You may need to cook the chicken in batches. Sauté the chicken until golden on one side, 2 to 3 minutes. Flip and sauté until lightly golden on the other side, about 2 minutes. Transfer the chicken to a plate. The chicken is par-cooked at this point, *donta* you worry.

Add the shallots to the pan and sauté until tender, about 1 minute. If the pan is dry, add another tablespoon (15 ml) oil.

Add the chicken stock, lemon peel, lemon juice, lemon slices and capers. Return the chicken to the pan, nestling it into the sauce. Reduce the heat to medium-low and finish cooking the chicken, 2 to 3 minutes, flipping the chicken halfway through cooking. Transfer the chicken to a platter. Cut the heat.

Add the butter into the sauce and constantly swirl the pan until the butter is melted, 1 to 2 minutes. Don't break the sauce (see Chefie Tip on page 25). Season to taste with salt and pepper. Pour the sauce over the chicken. Let the chicken rest, 5 minutes. Garnish with parsley, because you're fancy.

WILD MUSHROOM CHICKEN MARSALA

Don't skimp on the marsala wine; it doesn't have to be expensive but it needs to be good, no imitations. It'll make a difference, giving it a fortified, slightly sweet, rich flavor.

SERVES 3 TO 4

3 to 4 boneless skinless chicken breasts (1½ pounds [680 g]) - pounded even and dried well

kosher salt

fresh finely ground black pepper

⅓ cup (41 g) all-purpose flour

3 tablespoons (45 ml) avocado oil

4 tablespoons (56 g) cold unsalted butter - divided

9 ounces (255 g) cremini, shiitake and oyster mushrooms - wiped clean, sliced

1 medium shallot - minced (about 3 tablespoons [3 g])

4 garlic cloves - minced

½ cup (120 ml) marsala wine

1 cup (240 ml) Homemade Chicken Stock (page 169)

½ cup (120 ml) heavy cream

2 tablespoons (4 g) chopped fresh tarragon or Italian parsley

Season the chicken with 1¼ teaspoons (7.5 g) salt and ½ teaspoon pepper. Dredge the chicken on both sides in the flour, shaking off the excess. Set aside.

Heat a 12-inch (30.5-cm) frying pan over medium-high heat. Add the oil. When the oil shimmers, add the chicken and sear until lightly golden brown, about 2 minutes on each side. Transfer the chicken to a plate.

In the same pan over medium heat, melt 3 tablespoons (42 g) *buttah*. Add the mushrooms and season with ¾ teaspoon salt and ¼ teaspoon pepper. Sauté until tender and golden, 5 to 6 minutes. Add the shallots and garlic, and sauté until tender and you can smell the *gálick*, about 1 minute.

Remove the pan from heat. Add the marsala, return the pan back to the heat (be careful of flare-ups) and deglaze until reduced by one-third, 30 to 40 seconds. Pour in the chicken stock and heavy cream, season with ¼ teaspoon salt and a pinch of pepper and stir to combine. Reduce the heat to medium-low and simmer.

Return the chicken to the pan and cook until tender and just cooked through, 4 to 6 minutes, turning the chicken halfway through cooking. Cradle the heat between medium and medium-low. Don't overcook it. Remove the chicken and divide it among three to four plates, or place it on a medium platter; keep warm. Continue simmering the sauce over medium-low heat until thickened, 3 to 6 minutes.

If you want the sauce a little thicker, knead 1 tablespoon (8 g) flour into the remaining 1 tablespoon (14 g) cold butter, making a paste (see Chefie Tip for beurre manié on page 112). Otherwise, if it's the consistency you like, just finish with the remaining 1 tablespoon (14 g) cold butter, stirring until melted off the heat. Don't break the sauce (see Chefie Tip on page 25). Divide the marsala sauce over the chicken breasts. Garnish with tarragon or parsley, because you're fancy.

CACIO E PEPE

This dish is all about technique, with practice you'll master it quickly. It's a traditional Roman dish best prepared with good-quality ingredients, which is crucial, since you've only got three, so make 'em count. A dry, high-starch spaghetti is commonly used, but I wanted to put my homemade pasta (page 153) to the test, and it worked flawlessly, delivering a tender and uber creamy, peppered pasta dish. Make the pasta up to two days ahead, and keep it covered in the refrigerator. Then you can whip this dish up quickly.

SERVES 2 TO 3

2 cups (200 g) fresh finely grated Italian Pecorino Romano (see Chefie Tips)

½ tablespoon (6 g) black peppercorns - divided

½ pound (227 g) fresh homemade spaghetti (page 153)

CHEFIE TIP

Use a microplane to grate the Pecorino Romano for a feathery-light and airy texture.

In a 4-quart (3.5-L) pot over medium-high heat, bring 5 cups (1.2 L) salted water to a rolling bubble. You'll only need 4 to 4½ (960 ml to 1 L) cups of this water through the prepping and cooking process. I'm giving you extra for safety.

In a medium bowl, add the Pecorino Romano and pour in 1 ladle of hot salted water, stirring with a rubber spatula, making a paste (it should look like mashed potatoes). Set aside.

Using a mortar and pestle, roughly crack all the peppercorns, making some shattered and some finely ground. Set aside ½ teaspoon to garnish.

In a 12-inch (30.5-cm) slope-sided frying pan over low heat, add 1 teaspoon cracked peppercorns, and lightly toast until warm and fragrant, about 2 minutes, swirling the pan. Ladle all (except for 1 cup [240 ml]) of the salted water into the pan with the pepper. Increase the heat to medium-high and bring to a steady gentle bubble. Immediately add the pasta to the pan, making sure it's just covered in the water. Continue boiling while gently but vigorously stirring the pasta in the water and swirling the pan, using a rubber spatula so you don't break the fresh pasta. The pasta will slowly release its starch while the water reduces, creating a thickened opaque consistency. Once the water is reduced by three-quarters, about 2 minutes, remove the pan from the heat.

Add the Pecorino Romano paste to the pan, and constantly stir the pasta and swirl the pan until the cheese is fully melted and creamy, about 1 minute. Let it sit, 30 seconds, and divide the pasta among two to three bowls, along with the cheese sauce from the pan. Garnish with more freshly grated Pecorino Romano and the reserved black pepper, because you're a feisty rockstar chef.

HOT OFF THE GRILL OR GRIDDLE

Charred flavah can be achieved on the grill or on the griddle.

33

SPATCHCOCK CHICKEN WITH ZA'ATAR TAHINI

Za'atar is a Middle Eastern spice blend. I know, I mispronounced it in my video, ugh. It's ZAH-tar. Out of respect I do not like to mispronounce anything, plus when it's pronounced correctly, it sounds sexy . . . just like this aromatic, spiced, creamy sauce drizzled over this juicy chicken.

SERVES 4

1 (4-pound [1.8-kg]) whole chicken

avocado oil

kosher salt

fresh finely ground black pepper

1 lemon - halved

ZA'ATAR TAHINI

1 garlic clove - finely grated

zest of 1 lemon - finely grated

¼ cup (60 ml) freshly squeezed lemon juice

1 cup (240 ml) 5% or 2% Greek yogurt

½ cup (120 ml) tahini

1½ teaspoons (1.5 g) za'atar

¼ teaspoon cayenne pepper

½ cup (120 ml) milk

3 tablespoons (17 g) chopped fresh mint - to garnish

¼ cup (4 g) chopped fresh cilantro - to garnish

Heat one side of the grill over medium heat for 15 minutes. Remove the chicken from the refrigerator and bring to room temperature, 30 minutes. Remove the neck and giblets from the chicken, discarding the giblets. Toss the neck into a large zipper bag to freeze for stock (page 169).

Place the chicken breast side down. Using kitchen shears, cut and remove the backbone. Toss the backbone in the same bag with the neck. Flip the chicken over and give it a gentle push at the neck to flatten. Dry the chicken really well with heavy-duty paper towels to prevent it from sticking to the grill. Lightly rub the entire chicken with a thin coating of oil. Season the chicken generously on both sides with salt and pepper.

Oil the grill grates. Place the chicken skin side down on the grill. Add a grill press or a heavy cast-iron skillet to weigh it down. Sear, 2 minutes, turn it 90 degrees and sear, another 2 minutes, to create cross-hatch marks. Cradle the heat between medium and medium-high. Don't burn it. Flip the chicken and transfer skin side up onto a rimmed baking sheet. Place the baking sheet on the cold side of the grill and close the lid. Cook the chicken until just cooked through, 30 to 35 minutes. Remove the chicken to rest, 10 minutes.

Meanwhile, grill the halved lemon until slightly charred, 30 seconds to 1 minute. Remove to a medium serving platter.

TO MAKE THE ZA'ATAR TAHINI: In a medium bowl, stir garlic, lemon zest and lemon juice and let set, 1 minute. It mellows the *gálick*. Add the yogurt, tahini, za'atar, cayenne, ¾ teaspoon salt and ¼ teaspoon pepper and whisk to combine. The sauce will be thick. Slowly add the milk while whisking to thin for a loose yet saucy consistency. Transfer the sauce to a clean bowl.

Cut up the chicken, removing the breasts, thighs, legs and wings, and place them on the platter with the grilled lemon. Place the chicken carcass into the bag with the neck and backbone. Garnish with mint and cilantro, because you're fancy like that.

Use the grilled lemon for squeezing over the chicken and place za'atar tahini sauce alongside the platter to drizzle over the chicken.

SPICE-RUBBED BABY BACK RIBS WITH CHIPOTLE BARBECUE SAUCE

Starting the ribs in the oven then finishing them on the grill for a reverse sear gives that charred grilled flavor, while keeping the ribs moist and incredibly tender. No need to caramelize the barbecue sauce directly on the grill; sounds good in theory, but it's not worth the insane headache to clean the grill grates for hoursssss after. I've got an easier way.

SERVES 4

1 tablespoon (7 g) paprika

2 teaspoons (5 g) granulated garlic

2 teaspoons (4 g) ground cumin

½ teaspoon cayenne pepper

2 tablespoons (28 g) packed light brown sugar

kosher salt

fresh finely ground black pepper

2 racks (2½ to 3 pounds [1.3 to 1.4 kg] each) pork baby back ribs

2 to 3 tablespoons (30 to 45 ml) canola oil + more for oiling

2 cups (480 ml) Chipotle Barbecue Sauce (recipe follows)

Heat the oven to 400°F (204°C).

In a small bowl, combine paprika, granulated garlic, cumin, cayenne, *shugá*, 3 teaspoons (18 g) salt and ½ teaspoon pepper.

Using the tip of a paring knife, release the membrane from the ribs. Using a heavy-duty paper towel, grab the membrane, pull and rip it away to remove it. Dry the ribs very well with heavy-duty paper towels. Drizzle 2 to 3 tablespoons (30 to 45 ml) oil over the ribs on both sides.

Using clean, dry hands, massage the spice rub evenly all over both sides of the ribs. Place the ribs meat side up on a rimmed baking sheet. Add 1½ cups (360 ml) water to the bottom of the baking sheet. Cover and tightly seal the baking sheet with two pieces of foil, slightly overlapping so it's completely covered. Bake until the ribs are uber tender but still intact on the bone (almost all of the water will have evaporated), about 1 hour 30 minutes.

Heat the grill over medium heat, 10 to 15 minutes. Remove the ribs from the oven and let them rest, 5 to 8 minutes. Cut each rack in half between the bones, making four portions.

Reduce the heat of the grill; maintaining between medium-low to low, while grilling. Place two pieces of foil over one side of the grill. Oil the grates on the non-foiled side of the grill, and lightly oil the ribs. Place the ribs, meat side down, on the grill grates. Sear until lightly charred, 1 to 1½ minutes. Don't burn 'em. Turn the ribs 90 degrees, and continue searing, another minute. Flip the ribs and grill, grabbing more smokey flavor from the grill, 1 to 2 minutes.

(continued)

SPICE-RUBBED BABY BACK RIBS WITH CHIPOTLE BARBECUE SAUCE *(continued)*

Transfer the ribs to the foil side of the grill and lower the heat to low. Brush 1 cup (240 ml) barbecue sauce all over the ribs on both sides. With the ribs meat side up, lower the grill lid to caramelize the barbecue sauce, 3 to 5 minutes. Serve the remaining barbecue sauce on the side for dipping.

CHIPOTLE BARBECUE SAUCE

MAKES ABOUT 2¾ CUPS (660 ML)

1 tablespoon (15 ml) avocado or canola oil

⅓ cup (50 g) diced yellow onion

3 garlic cloves - minced

1 cup (240 ml) tomato paste

zest of ½ orange - finely grated

¾ cup (180 ml) freshly squeezed orange juice

½ cup (55 g) packed light brown sugar

⅓ cup (80 ml) apple cider vinegar

⅓ cup (80 ml) unsulphured molasses (not robust)

¼ cup (60 ml) light corn syrup

¼ cup (60 ml) less-sodium soy sauce

4 chipotles in adobo - minced, + 2 tablespoons (30 ml) adobo sauce

1 tablespoon (7 g) smoked paprika

¼ teaspoon cayenne pepper

¾ teaspoon kosher salt

¼ teaspoon fresh finely ground black pepper

Heat the oil in a 2-quart (1.9-L) pot over medium heat. Sauté the onions until tender and lightly caramelized, 4 to 5 minutes. Sauté the *gálick* until you can smell it, about 1 minute. Add the tomato paste and cook, stirring constantly with a rubber spatula, until caramelized, 3 to 4 minutes. It deepens the flavor.

Add the orange zest, orange juice, brown sugar, apple cider vinegar, molasses, corn syrup, soy sauce, chipotles, adobo sauce, paprika, cayenne, salt and pepper, and whisk until smooth. Bring the mixture to a gentle bubble over medium-high heat. Reduce the heat and simmer to build all the flavors, 15 to 20 minutes, stirring occasionally.

Remove the pot from the heat. Transfer the sauce to a blender and puree until smooth. Let the sauce cool to room temperature. Cover and refrigerate, up to 1 week.

SALMON BURGERS WITH FENNEL SLAW

This will be the best salmon burger you've ever had and if you don't like salmon, just give this a try. It's layered with delicious, fresh flavors. The key here: Don't overcook the salmon and just know cooking fish outside on the grill in a pan works like a charm and keeps the smells out of the kitchen.

MAKES 4 BURGERS

FOR THE LEMON VINAIGRETTE

2 tablespoons (2 g) chopped shallot

¼ cup (60 ml) freshly squeezed lemon juice

⅓ cup (80 ml) extra virgin olive oil

1 tablespoon (15 ml) honey

1 tablespoon (15 ml) Dijon mustard

kosher salt

fresh finely ground black pepper

FOR THE FENNEL SLAW

1 small bulb fennel - cored and thinly shaved

3 tablespoons (10 g) chopped fresh dill

MAKE THE LEMON VINAIGRETTE: In a small blender, add the shallot, lemon juice, olive oil, honey, Dijon, ½ teaspoon salt and ⅛ teaspoon pepper and blend until smooth. (Do not add the honey first, it'll stick to the bottom of the blender.) Reserve and set aside ¼ cup (60 ml) of the vinaigrette.

Pour the remaining vinaigrette into a medium bowl.

MAKE THE FENNEL SLAW: In the same bowl with the vinaigrette, add the fennel and dill, season with ½ teaspoon salt, and toss.

(continued)

SALMON BURGERS WITH FENNEL SLAW

(continued)

FOR THE SALMON BURGERS

1¼ pounds (565 g) wild king salmon - skin removed, cut into large chunks

⅓ cup (17 g) chopped fresh dill

¼ cup (27 g) Italian-style breadcrumbs

2 tablespoons (30 ml) avocado oil

½ cup (120 ml) homemade mayonnaise (page 160)

2 tablespoons (30 ml) Dijon mustard

2 tablespoons (30 ml) honey

4 tablespoons (56 g) unsalted butter - room temperature

4 Brioche Burger Buns (page 143)

kale leaves

MAKE THE SALMON BURGERS: In a food processor fitted with the blade attachment, add the salmon, reserved ¼ cup (60 ml) vinaigrette, dill, breadcrumbs, ¾ teaspoon salt and ¼ teaspoon pepper. Pulse until the mixture is finely minced, not whipped. Divide and form the salmon mixture into patties. They'll seem a tad wet, *donta* you worry; when cooked they'll form, holding their shape.

Heat the grill over medium heat.

Once the grill is well heated, place a 12-inch (30.5-cm) nonstick frying pan over the grates and add the oil. Heat the oil for 1 minute. Add the salmon burgers and cook until golden brown, just cooked through and juicy, 2 to 3 minutes on each side. Cradle the heat between medium and medium-low. Don't burn 'em. Remove the burgers and let them rest, 5 minutes. Alternatively, you can cook the burgers inside on the stove.

In a small bowl, stir the mayonnaise, Dijon mustard and honey until blended.

Spread a thin layer of butter on each of the bun halves and lightly toast them on the grill, about 30 seconds. Be careful of flare-ups.

Spread the mayonnaise mixture on the bottom bun, top with kale leaves, salmon burger, fennel slaw and close with top bun. Repeat with the remaining burgers.

CHEFIE TIP

You can make the patties up to 6 hours ahead; cover the patties and refrigerate until ready to grill. Remove from the refrigerator to remove the chill, 20 minutes ahead. If you are making these ahead, do not add the salt and pepper until ready to cook.

GRILLED SAUSAGE AND PEPPERONI PIZZA

One of my first jobs when I was 13 years old was working at a pizza shop. Although I managed the hoagie station and made cheesesteaks, I can make a mean pizza pie, too! If you'd like to cook your toppings inside on the stove, go for it! Or if you wanna enjoy cooking al fresco, my directions below guide you through. Alternatively, you can make this on a pizza stone in your oven.

MAKES 2 (14-INCH [35.5-CM]) PIZZAS; SERVES 6 TO 8

1 tablespoon (15 ml) olive oil + more for brushing

1 small onion - diced

3 garlic cloves - minced

1 pound (454 g) Italian sausage - casings removed

1¼ teaspoon (1.25 g) dried oregano

kosher salt

fresh finely ground black pepper

all-purpose flour

2 homemade pizza dough balls (page 150)

Heat one side of the grill over medium-high heat and the other side over medium heat.

Once the grill is well heated, add a 10-inch (25-cm) cast-iron skillet on the medium heated side of the grill and heat the pan. Add 1 tablespoon (15 ml) oil and the onions. Sauté the onions until tender crisp, about 2 minutes.

Add the garlic and sauté until you can smell the *gálick*, about 30 seconds. Add the sausage and dried oregano and lightly season with salt and pepper. Sauté the meat until fully browned, constantly breaking it up with a wooden spoon, 3 to 4 minutes. Remove from the grill and transfer the sausage to a bowl lined with paper towels, to absorb the excess oil. Lower the lid of the grill to create an oven effect.

Lightly brush a thin coating of olive oil onto a 14- or 16-inch (35.5- or 40.5-cm) pizza pan or baking sheet. The dough will be slightly sticky, *donta* you worry.

Working with one dough ball at a time, add a generous amount of flour into a wide bowl and place the dough ball into the bowl of flour, to coat the entire surface on both sides. Remove to a lightly floured, dusted surface and roll the dough out into a 13- to 14-inch (33- to 35.5-cm) circle. Place the dough on the pizza pan or baking sheet.

(continued)

GRILLED SAUSAGE AND PEPPERONI PIZZA

(continued)

2 cups (480 ml) homemade marinara (see Chefie Tip page 10) - divided

5 cups (560 g) freshly shredded whole-milk mozzarella - divided

40 to 60 thinly sliced pepperoni slices - divided

fresh oregano leaves - to garnish

Ladle half of the marinara over the pizza dough, leaving a 1-inch (2.5-cm) border for the crust. Sprinkle half of the cheese over the marinara and scatter half of the sausage and pepperoni slices.

Place the pizza pan or baking sheet on the medium heated side of the grill and lower the lid. Grill until the dough is cooked and lightly golden on the bottom and the cheese is melty, 10 to 14 minutes. Cradle the heat between medium and low as needed to control the browning on the bottom of the crust. Remove the pizza from the pizza pan or baking sheet with two large spatulas, a metal pizza peel or a thin, unrimmed cookie sheet and place the pizza directly onto the medium heated side of the grill grates. Lightly grill and crisp the bottom of the crust, about 30 seconds, turning if needed for even browning. Don't burn it!

Return the pizza back to the pizza pan or baking sheet and let it sit, 1 to 2 minutes off the grill. Garnish with fresh oregano, because you're fancy and cut into 6 slices.

Repeat with the second pizza pie.

CHEFIE TIPS

You can find inexpensive pizza sheet pans at restaurant supply stores, kitchen stores or online. Now you have your own outdoor pizza oven . . . on the grill (wink).

Wanna roll it out old-school? My video on Instagram or TikTok guides you through. Remember: I worked in a pizza shop for many years. This is way easier to do by hand, once you get the hang of it.

PATTY MELT WITH CARAMELIZED ONIONS

This is not a traditional patty melt but a damn good one. Insane actually. Instead of rye bread, we're using my homemade white bread. Yes, you must! And Dijon. Do not add thousand island dressing! I usually don't supersize food, but this one is an exception. You can use ground beef, but dialing it up by freshly grinding your own makes a better burger. Now, you'll know what's in your ground meat.

MAKES 2 SANDWICHES

6 tablespoons (84 g) unsalted butter - room temperature - divided

1 extra large Spanish onion - sliced

kosher salt

fresh finely ground black pepper

2 tablespoons (30 ml) cognac or brandy

1 pound (454 g) boneless beef chuck steak - cubed

1½ teaspoons (3.5 g) granulated garlic

1½ teaspoons (3.5 g) onion powder

Heat one side of the grill over medium-low heat and the other side over medium heat.

Once the grill is well heated, add a 10-inch (25.5-cm) cast-iron skillet over the medium-low heated side of the grill. Melt 2 tablespoons (28 g) *buttah* in the skillet. Add the onions and season with ¾ teaspoon salt and ¼ teaspoon pepper. Cook the onions, tossing occasionally, until caramelized, 25 to 30 minutes. Cradle the heat between medium-low and low.

Deglaze the pan with cognac until almost completely reduced, 20 to 30 seconds. Remove the skillet from the heat. Transfer the onion to a medium bowl and wipe the skillet clean. Keep the grill heated.

Grind the beef in a meat grinder or pulse/grind in a food processor fitted with the blade attachment. In a large bowl, add the ground beef, granulated *gálick*, onion powder, 1¼ teaspoons (7.5 g) salt and ½ teaspoon pepper. Using clean hands, mix the meat until combined. Divide and form 4 patties. Working with one at a time, place a piece of parchment paper over the patty and press using the back of a spatula, smashing the patty, making the same surface size area as the bread slices, until ¼ inch (6 mm) thick.

(continued)

PATTY MELT WITH CARAMELIZED ONIONS

(continued)

avocado oil

4 (½-inch [1-cm]) slices Old School White Sandwich Bread (page 146)

¼ cup (60 ml) Dijon mustard - divided

8 slices Swiss cheese - divided

deli-style dill pickles, for serving

Lightly drizzle avocado oil over the burger patties to moisten the spices and lightly coat the patties. Oil the medium heated grill grates. Place the burgers on the medium heated side of the grill, and cook until medium doneness, about 1½ minutes on each side, turning (not flipping) 90 degrees halfway through grilling to create cross-hatch marks. Transfer the burgers to a plate to keep warm.

Spread each slice of bread equally with the Dijon mustard.

To assemble: Add 2 slices of cheese on top of 1 slice of bread, 1 burger patty, a quarter of the caramelized onions, another burger patty on top, another slice of cheese, a quarter more of the onions, another slice of cheese and top with the second slice of bread, mustard side sandwiched down. Repeat with the second sandwich.

Spread the remaining 4 tablespoons (56 g) butter equally among the outside of each bread slice; working on parchment paper will be easier.

Place the cast-iron skillet over the medium-low heated side of the grill. Once the skillet is heated, add the assembled sandwiches into the skillet, buttered side down and toast until lightly golden and the cheese melts, 1 to 2 minutes on each side. Cradle the heat between medium-low to low. Lower the lid to fully melt the cheese. If the skillet is too crowded, cook one sandwich at a time.

Transfer the sandwiches to a cutting board. Cut the sandwiches in half on a diagonal and serve with dill pickles on the side for a traditional touch.

CHEFIE TIP

Don't have a meat grinder or food processor? Break out a chef's knife or cleaver and finely chop the meat.

GRILLED LAMB KOFTAS WITH HERBED LEMON YOGURT AND PICKLED ONIONS

Kofta or köfte are Middle Eastern–style spiced meatballs shaped like balls, patties or logs wrapped around skewers and grilled. Here's my take, served with grilled or warmed pita. I like to cook with olive oil and finish with extra virgin, so I call for both here.

SERVES 4

1 pound (454 g) ground lamb

¼ cup (40 g) grated yellow onion (about 1 extra small onion)

¼ cup (15 g) chopped fresh Italian parsley

2 large garlic cloves - finely grated

1 lemon - zest finely grated, then halved

2 tablespoons (11 g) chopped fresh mint

1½ teaspoons (3 g) ground cumin

¾ teaspoon ground cinnamon

kosher salt

fresh finely ground black pepper

FOR THE HERB LEMON YOGURT

1 (7-ounce [207-ml]) container 5% or 2% Greek yogurt

2 tablespoons (30 ml) freshly squeezed lemon juice

2 tablespoons (8 g) chopped fresh Italian parsley + more to garnish

1 tablespoon (6 g) chopped fresh mint + more to garnish

olive oil

If using wooden skewers, soak them in water for an hour to overnight.

In a large bowl, add the ground lamb, onions, parsley, garlic, lemon zest, mint, cumin, cinnamon, 1 teaspoon salt and ½ teaspoon pepper and mix very well until all the spices are evenly combined.

Spray skewers with nonstick cooking spray. Divide the meat evenly among four skewers, and tightly wrap the meat around each skewer into 6- to 7-inch- (15- to 18-cm-) long torpedoes. Place the skewers on parchment paper and chill in the refrigerator while making the herb yogurt. This will help congeal the fat to hold the meat on the skewer while grilling so it won't fall apart.

MAKE THE HERB LEMON YOGURT: In a small serving bowl, add the yogurt, lemon juice, parsley, mint and ¼ teaspoon salt. Stir until combined.

Heat the grill over medium heat.

Remove the koftas from the refrigerator and drizzle with a little olive oil on both sides.

Oil the grill grates. Place the koftas on the grill and cook until lightly charred and just cooked through, 10 to 12 minutes, turning on all four sides.

Add the halved lemon onto the grill, flesh side down to warm and lightly char, 1 to 2 minutes.

Transfer the koftas and lemons to a platter to rest, 5 minutes.

(continued)

GRILLED LAMB KOFTAS WITH HERBED LEMON YOGURT AND PICKLED ONIONS

(continued)

2 to 3 ripe tomatoes - cut into small wedges

Pickled Onions (recipe follows)

extra virgin olive oil

4 pocketless pitas - warmed

Arrange the tomatoes and some pickled onion slices around the koftas. Season the tomatoes with salt and pepper. Squeeze the grilled lemon over the koftas.

Drizzle a little extra virgin olive oil over everything. Garnish with extra parsley and mint, because you're fancy, and place the yogurt bowl on the platter.

To serve, wrap a warmed pita around a lamb skewer and pull to remove the skewer. Top with tomatoes, pickled onions, herbs and drizzle the herbed lemon yogurt over top.

PICKLED ONIONS

YIELDS 1 (32-OUNCE [946-ML]) JAR

1 cup (240 ml) rice wine vinegar

1 cup (240 ml) water

¼ cup (50 g) granulated sugar

1½ tablespoons (4 g) black peppercorns

1 tablespoon (15 g) kosher salt

2 medium red onions - thinly sliced into half moons

In a 32-oz (946-ml) Mason jar with a tight-fitted lid, add the vinegar, water, sugar, peppercorns and salt. Secure the lid and shake vigorously until the *shugá* and salt are dissolved. Add the onions. Jam 'em in there, don't break them. Pop the lid back on and shake. Store in your refrigerator, up to a week.

Top the onions on koftas, gyros, burgers, salads and sandwiches. They're delicious.

CHEFIE TIP

Prep the pickled onions several hours ahead or the day before, for best *flavah*.

STEAK SMASH BURGERS WITH POBLANO AIOLI

You're not even ready for this Poblano Aioli. Holy mackerel! It's insane. Making the homemade mayonnaise (page 160) is fast and easy if you have an immersion blender. Don't buy store-bought mayonnaise. Try it. It'll make the sauce over-the-top on this juicy steak burger.

MAKES 4 BURGERS

2 New York strip steaks (1¼ pounds [568 g] total) - cut into chunks

1 large white onion - sliced into half moons

1 large poblano chile

avocado oil or any neutral-flavored oil

kosher salt

fresh finely ground black pepper

1 garlic clove - finely grated

1 teaspoon to 2 tablespoons (5 to 30 ml) fresh lemon juice - divided (see Chefie Tips)

Place the steak cubes in the freezer for 10 minutes to blast-chill so it's not gummy when grinding.

Grind the steak in a meat grinder or in a food processor fitted with the blade attachment until finely ground. If using a food processor, pulse the meat until finely ground; don't whip it or the meat will get gummy. Clean the food processor if using. Leave the steak at room temperature while preparing everything else.

Adjust an oven rack to the top position. Heat the oven to broil.

Line a rimmed baking sheet with aluminum foil. Add the onion slices and whole poblano chile. Drizzle a little avocado oil over the onions and poblano. Season lightly with salt and pepper. Toss and broil until charred in spots, 6 to 7 minutes, turning the poblano halfway and tossing the onions periodically.

Transfer the poblano to a small bowl and cover with plastic wrap to steam, releasing the skin. Once it's cool enough to handle, peel away and discard the skin. Stem and de-seed the poblano. Roughly tear the poblano into pieces.

In a medium bowl, add the garlic and lemon juice and let it sit for 1 minute to mellow the *gálick*.

(continued)

STEAK SMASH BURGERS WITH
POBLANO AIOLI *(continued)*

1 cup (240 ml) homemade mayonnaise (page 160)

1 cup (15 g) fresh cilantro leaves and stems

zest of ½ lemon - finely grated

4 thick slices Monterey Jack or Pepper Jack cheese

4 Brioche Burger Buns (page 143), toasted (see Chefie Tips)

4 or more romaine lettuce leaves

1 large ripe tomato - sliced

CHEFIE TIPS

If you're using my homemade mayonnaise, only use 1 teaspoon (5 ml) lemon juice while following this recipe, otherwise it'll be too lemony and thin. If using store-bought, it'll need the 2 tablespoons (30 ml) of lemon juice.

To toast the Brioche Burger Buns (page 143), split the buns and spread with butter. Place the buns on the hot griddle or skillet until toasted.

In a food processor fitted with the blade attachment, add the mayonnaise, cilantro, poblano, ½ teaspoon salt and ¼ teaspoon pepper. Puree until chunky smooth. Stir in the lemon zest. Transfer to the bowl with the lemon and garlic and stir well. Refrigerate the aioli until ready to use. You can make this up to 2 days ahead; keep refrigerated.

Heat a griddle or 12-inch (30.5-cm) cast-iron skillet over medium to medium-high heat for 5 to 10 minutes. Cut a 5-inch (14-cm)-square piece of parchment paper.

Season the ground steak generously with salt and pepper. Divide and form the meat into 4 burger balls, 5 ounces (142 g) each.

Lightly drizzle the steak balls with avocado oil to evenly coat. Lightly drizzle avocado oil over the griddle or cast-iron skillet. When the oil is heated and shimmers, add 1 to 2 steak balls, depending on your surface area. Immediately place the parchment square directly on top, working with one at a time. With a spatula, quickly press to smash the ball into a ½-inch- (1-cm-) thick burger. Hold for 10 seconds to lock in the moisture and get a good sear. Remove the parchment square.

Cook, 2 to 2½ minutes on each side for medium doneness. During the last 30 seconds, add a slice of cheese on top of each burger and cover with a lid if needed to help melt the cheese. Transfer the burgers to a plate to rest and keep warm. Repeat with the remaining steak balls.

To assemble: Spread the poblano aioli on bottom burger bun, top with a romaine leaf, 1 smash burger and 1 tomato slice. Season with salt and pepper. Place the fried onions over the tomato, and smear more poblano aioli over the top bun to close.

GRILLED RACK OF LAMB WITH MINT PERSILLADE

Persillade, it's French! This is a sauce mixture of chopped parsley and garlic in olive oil. I also add mint and dill for a more rounded, herbaceous flavor and a touch of lemon for brightness.

SERVES 4

1 garlic clove - finely grated

zest of 1 small lemon - finely grated

2 teaspoons (10 ml) lemon juice

¼ cup (15 g) finely chopped fresh Italian parsley

¼ cup (23 g) finely chopped fresh mint

¼ cup (13 g) finely chopped fresh dill

⅔ cup (160 ml) good extra virgin olive oil

kosher salt

fresh finely ground black pepper

2 racks of lamb (1 to 1½ pounds [454 to 680 g] each) - frenched, excess fat trimmed and removed

avocado oil

fleur de sel or sea salt, to garnish

Make the mint persillade: In a small bowl, add the garlic and lemon zest. Stir in the lemon juice. It mellows the *gálick*. Add the parsley, mint, dill, olive oil, ½ teaspoon salt and ⅛ teaspoon pepper. Stir well to combine. You can make this up to 4 hours ahead and set at room temperature; place plastic wrap directly on top of the herb mixture to keep it nice and green.

Remove the lamb from the refrigerator and bring to room temperature, 30 minutes before grilling, to remove the chill. The last 15 minutes, heat one side of the grill over medium heat and the other side over medium-low heat. Tightly wrap the exposed bones with foil; this will prevent them from burning on the grill.

Drizzle a thin layer of avocado oil over the lamb and season with salt and pepper on both sides. Oil the grill grates and place both racks of lamb, meaty side down, on the medium heated side of the grill, with the bones not directly on the fire. Sear until brown, 2 minutes, turn 90 degrees (do not flip) and sear another 2 minutes, to create crosshatch marks. If flare-ups start, remove the lamb, die out the flames and return to the grill, controlling the flare-ups from the fat.

Flip and sear the other side until brown, about 2 minutes. Transfer both racks of lamb to the medium-low heated side of the grill, again with the bones not directly over the flame. Lower the lid, and continue grilling to medium-rare doneness, 10 to 15 minutes, or medium doneness, 12 to 18 minutes.

Transfer the racks of lamb to a cutting board and loosely tent with foil. Rest, 8 minutes. Slice the lamb between the bones into chops and divide and fan them out, slightly overlapping among four plates. Divide and drizzle the mint persillade over the lamb.

Garnish with fleur de sel or sea salt, because you're fancy.

CHEFIE TIP

Roll the lemon before squeezing; it loosens the juice.

CHIPOTLE BLACK BEAN BURGERS

If you're a meat lover, try these! They're loaded with tons of fresh, passionate flavors and are incredibly satisfying. You won't miss the beef. Cook pre-soaked dried black beans in a pressure cooker with your favorite aromatics and a touch of oil for 10 minutes, then quick release.

MAKES 4 BURGERS

3 tablespoons (45 ml) avocado oil - divided

1 small onion - chopped (about ½ cup [80 g])

kosher salt

3 garlic cloves - chopped

1¾ cups (258 g) cooked black beans (if using canned, drained and rinsed)

2 chipotle peppers in adobo - chopped

1 large egg - beaten

1½ teaspoons (3 g) ground cumin

1½ teaspoons (3.5 g) smoked paprika

1½ teaspoons (2.5 g) ground coriander

2 cups (16 g) fresh cilantro leaves - divided

fresh finely ground black pepper

⅓ cup (36 g) Italian breadcrumbs

4 tablespoons (56 g) unsalted butter - room temperature

4 Brioche Burger Buns (page 143)

1 lime - halved

1 ripe avocado - pitted and sliced

1 large ripe tomato - cut into 4 slices

In a 10-inch (25-cm) frying pan over medium heat, heat 1 tablespoon avocado oil. Add the onions and a pinch of salt. Sauté until tender and slightly caramelized, 2 to 3 minutes. Add the *gálick* and sauté until you can smell it, about 30 seconds. Cut the heat, let the mixture cool and transfer to a food processor fitted with the blade attachment.

Add the black beans, chipotles, egg, cumin, paprika, coriander, 1 cup (8 g) cilantro, 1 teaspoon salt and ¼ teaspoon pepper to the food processor with the onion. Pulse blend the mixture until chunky smooth, scraping down the sides of the bowl periodically. Fold in the breadcrumbs with a spatula and stir until the breadcrumbs are fully moistened. Divide and form the mixture into 4 patties.

Line a 14 x 12–inch (35.5 x 30.5–cm) baking sheet with aluminum foil and brush 1 tablespoon (15 ml) avocado oil over the foil. Place the burgers on top.

Heat the grill over medium heat.

When the grill is fully heated, gently transfer the foil sheet with the burgers directly on the grill. Drizzle the remaining 1 tablespoon (15 ml) avocado oil on top of the burgers. Grill until a crisp golden crust forms, 4 to 5 minutes. Flip. Be careful, they aren't quite fully set yet. Grill another 4 to 5 minutes until a crisp and golden crust forms. Transfer the burgers to a plate.

Spread the butter equally over each burger bun half and toast the buns on the grill, cut side down, 30 to 45 seconds. Don't burn 'em. Remove.

Place each burger on the bun bottoms. Squeeze lime halves over each burger. Divide and top with avocados, tomatoes and season with salt and pepper. Top with ¼ cup (4 g) cilantro on each burger. Close burger with the top bun.

BECAUSE YOU'RE LAZY

Takeout Sucks!

When you're too busy and want a quicker homemade meal, this is your go-to chapter.

MOM'S CHICKEN CUTLETS

This has been my go-to recipe once a week for more than twenty-five years. It's my son, Costas's, favorite and before that, my mom made it my whole life, growing up. We called it chicken cutlets, aka Chicken Milanese. It's incredibly easy and quick, and everyone loves it. Got stale bread? Use 'em up to make homemade breadcrumbs (see Chefie Tip below). Oh, and through my gazillion times of making these, I've found no flour is needed; it separates the coating from the chicken. Ditch it.

SERVES 3 TO 4

1¼ to 1½ pounds (568 to 680 g) organic boneless, skinless chicken breasts

⅔ cup (37 g) panko breadcrumbs

½ cup (28 g) Italian-style breadcrumbs

2 large eggs

1½ cups (360 ml) safflower or peanut oil

kosher salt

1 lemon - cut into wedges

1 tablespoon (4 g) chopped fresh Italian parsley

CHEFIE TIP

Tear stale bread into cubes and finely grind them in a food processor. If the crumbs are still a tad moist, spread them out on a rimmed baking sheet and bake at 225°F (107°C) for 20 to 30 minutes, tossing halfway until dried. Add 1 tablespoon (2 g) dried parsley and 1½ teaspoons (3.5 g) granulated garlic to the breadcrumbs. Adding the panko is optional, but I do like that they add an extra crispy texture.

Place the chicken breasts into a large zipper bag, push out all the air and zip to close. Using the flat side of a meat mallet, pound the chicken until they are all evenly ½ inch (1 cm) thick. Transfer the chicken to a plate.

In a wide, shallow bowl, toss the panko and Italian-style breadcrumbs. In another wide, shallow bowl, whisk the eggs.

Dredge the chicken on both sides in the egg wash, dripping off the excess. Then dredge and press into the breadcrumb mixture to fully adhere on both sides, gently shaking off any excess. Set the chicken aside on a plate. You can prep the chicken up to several hours ahead and keep refrigerated until ready to cook.

Heat a 12-inch (30.5-cm) frying pan over medium heat. Add the oil and heat until it shimmers, 2 to 3 minutes. Add the chicken. Pan-fry until golden brown, 3 to 4 minutes. If the breadcrumbs are browning too quickly, reduce and cradle the heat between medium to medium-low, as needed, so they don't burn. Flip and pan-fry the other side until golden and the chicken is just cooked through, 2 to 3 minutes. Don't overcook it!

Transfer the chicken to a wire rack over a rimmed sheet pan and immediately season generously with salt over top. It'll season the coating and through to the chicken. This is the only time I season protein after cooked. Let it rest, about 8 minutes.

Squeeze fresh lemon juice over the chicken and garnish with parsley, because you're fancy!

PAN-SEARED NEW YORK STRIP STEAK WITH CABERNET PAN SAUCE

You only need ¼ cup (60 ml) cabernet to make the sauce, but grab a good one, a really good one; it'll make a difference, then you can enjoy the rest of the bottle with your steak dinner. Even though tonight you're feeling lazy, you can still be fancy (wink).

SERVES 2

2 boneless New York strip steaks (1 to 1½ inch [2.5 to 3.8 cm] thick)

kosher salt

fresh finely ground black pepper

2 tablespoons (30 ml) avocado oil

1 tablespoon (1 g) minced shallot

2 tablespoons (4 g) fresh thyme leaves

¼ cup (60 ml) good cabernet

¾ cup (180 ml) Homemade Beef Stock (page 170)

2 tablespoons (28 g) cold unsalted butter

1 tablespoon (4 g) fresh Italian parsley - finely chopped, to garnish

Remove the steaks from the refrigerator for 30 minutes before cooking, to remove the chill. Place them on a heavy-duty paper towel-lined plate and place a couple heavy-duty paper towels on top of the steaks to dry them really well. That way you can get a good sear; moisture is the enemy. Season generously with salt and desired amount of pepper on both sides.

Heat a 10- or 12-inch (25.5- or 30.5-cm) heat-safe frying pan, 1 to 2 minutes (choose the pan that comfortably fits the steaks). Add the oil and heat it, 15 seconds. Add the steaks. Don't touch 'em. For a boneless 1-inch- (2.5-cm-) thick steak, sear until evenly browned, 4 minutes per inch per side for medium-rare. For medium doneness, after searing place the heat-safe pan into a 400°F (204°C) oven, 2 to 2½ minutes. For a boneless 1½-inch- (3.8-cm-) thick steak, sear until evenly browned, 3 to 4 minutes on each side, then place into a 400°F (204°C) oven, 2 to 4 minutes for medium-rare. For medium doneness, add a couple more minutes. Remove the steaks from the pan and let them rest, 5 minutes.

Degrease the pan, if needed, leaving 1 to 2 tablespoons (15 to 30 ml) oil. Heat the pan over medium heat. Add the shallots and thyme. The thyme will pop, *donta* you worry. Sauté the shallots until tender, 30 seconds. Deglaze with wine and reduce slightly, 20 to 30 seconds. Whisk in the beef stock, breaking up the fond (little brown bits at the bottom of the pan, it's French). Cradle the heat between medium and medium-low until the liquid is reduced by half, 5 to 6 minutes. Don't over-reduce it. Once you see bubbles steadily break the entire surface, cut the heat. Stir in the butter while swirling the pan at the same time until melted. Don't break the sauce! Taste it. Season with salt and pepper to your liking. Let the sauce rest for a couple minutes to further thicken. Slice steaks on a bias into ½-inch (1-cm) slices crosswise. Pour the pan sauce over both steaks and garnish with parsley, because you're fancy.

QUESO FLAMEADO

Queso Flameado means flamed cheese. It's Mexican! A dish of hot melted cheese and chorizo flambéed table side and served like fondue. Since we're not in a restaurant, there's no need for a fancy table-side show. I flambé before adding the cheese to get that delicious, concentrated smoky tequila flavor. If you don't want to flambé, *donta* you worry. Just skip it and reduce to burn off the alcohol. This dish is typically served as an appetizer, but I like to make tacos with the queso and eat it for dinner.

SERVES 4 TO 6

2 poblano chiles

1 tablespoon (15 ml) avocado oil

½ cup (80 g) diced yellow or white onion

½ pound (227 g) chorizo - casing removed

¼ cup (60 ml) reposado tequila

10 ounces (283 g) Monterey Jack cheese - freshly shredded (about 2½ cups)

10 ounces (283 g) Oaxaca cheese - freshly shredded (about 2½ cups)

2 limes - divided

2 Fresno or serrano chiles - sliced

⅓ cup (5 g) roughly chopped fresh cilantro

12 Handmade Corn Tortillas (page 163) - toasted (see Chefie Tip)

CHEFIE TIP

Toast the tortillas on an open flame or on the grill until lightly charred. Wrap them in foil and keep warm until ready to serve or they'll dry out.

Adjust the oven rack to the top position. Heat the broiler on high.

Line a small rimmed baking sheet with aluminum foil. Add the poblanos. Broil until they are evenly blackened and charred, about 8 minutes, turning a couple times.

Transfer the poblanos to a large bowl. Cover them with plastic wrap and set aside to steam, loosening the skin. Once they are cool enough to handle, peel and discard the skin. Remove the stem and seeds and dice the poblanos.

Return the oven rack to the center position. Heat the oven to 375°F (190°C).

In a 10-inch (30.5-cm) cast-iron skillet over high heat, heat the oil. Add the onion and chorizo, and sauté until browned, about 5 minutes, breaking up the chorizo into small crumbles. Reduce the heat to medium. Stir in the diced poblanos.

Deglaze with tequila until reduced by a third, about 15 seconds. Don't fully burn it off, we want that oaky flavor. Add the Monterey Jack and Oaxaca cheeses and roughly stir, mixing it through the chorizo, keeping the majority of the cheese on top.

Bake until hot, melted and bubbly, 12 to 14 minutes. Remove the queso from the oven and squeeze half of 1 lime over top.

Garnish with Fresno or serrano chiles and cilantro. Serve immediately from the skillet. Use the tortilla to pinch and scoop the queso on the tortilla the authentic way and eat it like a taco. Serve with the remaining lime cut into wedges on the side for squeezing.

WEEKNIGHT CHILI

This is my go-to recipe when I'm too busy to grind the meat. Ha, yes, sometimes I'm lazy too (wink). Have more time and want the beefed-up version? Grind chuck steak and see the Chefie Tip below for pressure-cooked beans. If you'd like to use store-bought stock here, I'd rather you use chicken stock. Store-bought beef stock is nasty.

SERVES 6

1½ tablespoons (23 ml) canola oil

1 small onion - diced

kosher salt

fresh finely ground black pepper

3 garlic cloves - minced

1 pound (454 g) 85% lean ground beef

2½ teaspoons (6 g) chili powder

1½ teaspoons (3 g) ground cumin

1½ teaspoon (3 g) ancho chili powder

½ teaspoon smoked paprika

¼ teaspoon cayenne pepper

1 (15-ounce [439-g]) can small red kidney beans - drained and rinsed

1¾ cups (411 g) jar canned tomatoes (page 140) or 1 (14.5-ounce [411-g]) can fire-roasted diced tomatoes

1 cup (240 ml) Homemade Chicken Stock (page 169) or Homemade Beef Stock (page 170)

sour cream

1 jalapeño - thinly sliced

1 lime - cut into wedges

fresh cilantro leaves

In a 4-quart (3.8-L) Dutch oven over medium heat, heat the oil. Add the onions, ¼ teaspoon salt and ⅛ teaspoon pepper. Sauté until the onions are tender, 3 to 4 minutes. Add the garlic and sauté until you can smell it, about 30 seconds.

Add the beef. Season with 1½ teaspoons (9 g) salt and ¾ teaspoon pepper. Sauté, breaking up the meat with a wooden spoon, over medium-high heat until evenly browned, about 5 minutes. Sprinkle the chili powder, cumin, ancho chili powder, paprika and cayenne over the meat and sauté until the spices are toasted, 1 to 2 minutes.

Stir in the beans, tomatoes and chicken or beef stock. Bring to a slight bubble, then reduce the heat to simmer. Cover and cook until the meat is tender, 35 to 50 minutes. The longer you simmer the meat, the more tender it will be. Remove the lid and continue cooking over medium-low heat to reduce some of the liquid, 8 to 10 minutes more (your texture should be more stew-like when stirred, less soupy).

Remove from the heat and stir. Let rest to further thicken, about 8 minutes. Taste it and season to taste with salt and pepper.

Divide among bowls. Top each bowl with a dollop of sour cream, jalapeños (as desired) and serve lime wedges on the side for squeezing over top. Garnish with cilantro, because you're fancy.

CHEFIE TIP

Pressure-cook on HIGH presoaked dried small red kidney beans in 8 cups (1.9 L) water with a touch of oil and some aromatics for 8 minutes, then allow to naturally release.

GRILLED SALT AND PEPPER CHICKEN WITH HAZELNUT PESTO

My friend Jeannette calls grilled or sautéed chicken seasoned with salt and pepper, salt and pepper chicken and that's exactly what this is. Good organic chicken, in my opinion, tastes better and is juicer, so all it needs is salt and pepper. But don't overcook it or it'll be dry. When you cut the chicken after resting, the juices should run clear. Yes, it should be juicy! No need to add spices; instead pair it with other layers, like my hazelnut pesto, to build flavor.

SERVES 4

3 organic boneless, skinless chicken breasts (about 1½ pounds [680 g])

2 tablespoons (30 ml) avocado oil + more for oiling

kosher salt

fresh finely ground black pepper

FOR THE HAZELNUT PESTO

⅓ cup (38 g) shelled hazelnuts - toasted

3 garlic cloves - minced

3 tablespoons (45 ml) lemon juice

4 cups (160 g) packed fresh basil leaves

kosher salt

fresh finely ground black pepper

1 cup (240 ml) good extra virgin olive oil

¾ cup (180 ml) fresh finely grated Parmigiano-Reggiano

Heat the grill or a cast-iron grill pan over medium heat, 10 to 15 minutes.

Place the chicken into a large zipper bag, press out the air and zip to close. Evenly pound the chicken, making the breasts ½ inch (1 cm) thick. Transfer the chicken to a plate and set aside at room temperature, 20 to 30 minutes, to remove the chill. Evenly drizzle the chicken with 2 tablespoons (30 ml) oil on both sides and season with 1½ teaspoons (3.5 g) salt and ½ teaspoon pepper on both sides.

Rub the grill grates with oil. Grill the chicken, 4 to 4½ minutes, turning 90 degrees halfway through cooking to create crosshatch marks. Flip the chicken and grill until just cooked through, 4 minutes more, turning 90 degrees halfway through cooking to create cross-hatch marks. Cradle the heat between medium and medium-low, depending on how hot your grill gets. You want nicely golden grill marks. Transfer the chicken to a plate to rest, 8 minutes.

MAKE THE HAZELNUT PESTO: In a food processor, add the hazelnuts and pulse until finely chopped. Add the garlic to the processor. Squeeze the lemon juice over the garlic and stir. It mellows the *gálick*. Add the basil, 1¼ teaspoons (3 g) salt and ¼ teaspoon pepper. Puree while adding the oil through the feed tube. Stop the food processor from time to time, pushing the basil down until evenly blended. Continue pureeing until chunky smooth. Don't make this in a blender; it'll make the texture too smooth. Stir in the Parmigiano-Reggiano.

Slice the chicken and serve the hazelnut pesto drizzled over top.

WHOLE ROASTED FISH WITH HERB-LEMON OIL

Don't be intimidated by making whole fish. It's the easiest thing you'll ever make. It's super moist, tender and cooks fast. Be patient, practice makes perfect when filleting it, and with each time you'll get better and better, if you're not already a pro.

I can eat whole fish every day. It's fresh, simple and deliciously sexy. Pair it with a salad, roasted or fried potatoes and a good bottle of white wine. Now, that's livin'!

If preparing a fish that weighs 2 to 2½ pounds (908 g to 1.1 kg), roast it in the oven, 20 to 25 minutes. One fish will serve two.

SERVES 2

2 (1- to 1¼-pound [454- to 568-g]) whole branzino, black bass or red snapper - scaled, gutted, gills removed

kosher salt

fresh finely ground black pepper

fresh dill

1 medium shallot - quartered

1 small lemon - thinly sliced

extra virgin olive oil

FOR THE HERB LEMON OIL

⅓ cup (80 ml) good extra virgin olive oil

¼ cup (60 ml) freshly squeezed lemon juice

1 extra-small shallot - chopped

¾ teaspoon granulated sugar

2 tablespoons (7 g) finely chopped fresh dill

2 tablespoons (8 g) finely chopped fresh Italian parsley

fleur de sel or sea salt, to garnish

Heat the oven to 425°F (218°C).

Line a rimmed baking sheet with parchment paper. Spray the parchment with nonstick cooking spray.

Season the cavity of both fish with salt and pepper and stuff with small bunches of dill, the shallots and lemon slices. Rub the outside of both fish with a thin layer of oil and season lightly with salt and pepper on both sides.

Place the fish on the prepared baking sheet. Place the baking sheet in the oven on the center rack and roast until cooked through (internal temperature of 160°F [71°C]), 12 to 15 minutes.

Remove the fish from the oven and let it rest, 8 minutes.

FOR THE HERB LEMON OIL, in a blender, combine the olive oil, lemon juice, shallots and *shugá* and puree until smooth. Stir in ¾ teaspoon salt, the dill and parsley. Taste the sauce and season lightly with additional salt and pepper, if needed.

Using two forks and a small spatula, fillet the fish, discarding the skin. Save the head and pick through it, if it doesn't freak you out. There's a lot of good meat in there.

Divide the fish among two plates. Drizzle your desired amount of herb lemon oil over the fish. Lightly season with fleur del sel or sea salt, because you're fancy.

SHRIMP FRIED RICE (*NASI GORENG UDANG*)

Nasi Goreng is Indonesia's national dish. Here's my take using shrimp. You can find bird's eye chilis at most Asian markets and online, or substitute for dried chile de árbol or Fresno chile. Takara mirin can also be found online. Splitting the chile versus mincing controls the heat, so you aren't biting into a minced chile which causes the spice to ignite, overpowering the dish. Plus, it makes it pretty.

Feeling extra lazy and have leftover cooked Salt and Pepper Chicken (page 68) or Pan-Seared New York Strip Steak (page 63)? Substitute the shrimp with either. Just add it at the end to warm it through.

SERVES 2 TO 3

1 pound (454 g) wild shrimp (U/21 to U/25) - peeled, deveined, tails removed

kosher salt

fresh finely ground black pepper

6 tablespoons (90 ml) avocado, canola or peanut oil - divided

2 to 4 fresh Thai bird's eye chilis - split

5 garlic cloves - minced

1½ tablespoons (9 g) peeled, minced ginger

4 to 5 green onions - sliced, whites and dark greens separated

2 large eggs

2 cups (372 g) leftover rice (see Chefie Tip)

2 tablespoons (30 ml) less-sodium soy sauce

2 tablespoons (30 ml) mirin (Takara mirin preferred)

Season the shrimp with ½ teaspoon salt and ¼ teaspoon pepper. Heat a wok or 12-inch (30.5-cm) frying pan over medium-high heat, 30 seconds to 1 minute. Add 2 tablespoons (30 ml) oil. When the oil is heated and shimmers, add the shrimp, bird's eye chilis, garlic, ginger and the whites of the green onions. Stir-fry until the shrimp are just cooked through, 1 to 2 minutes. Transfer the shrimp and all the aromatics to a large bowl.

Add 2 more tablespoons (30 ml) oil to the wok or frying pan. Add the eggs and scramble until well done, 1 to 1½ minutes. Add the rice and 1 to 2 more tablespoons (15 to 30 ml) oil and season lightly with salt and pepper. Stir-fry until the rice is toasty and slightly crispy, 2 to 3 minutes. Make sure the rice is not wet. If it is, keep stir-frying.

Add the soy sauce and mirin. Stir-fry until completely reduced and absorbed into the rice and the rice is toasty (not wet), 1½ to 2 minutes. Return the shrimp along with the aromatics to the pan and warm through, 30 seconds. Transfer the stir-fry to a medium serving platter. Garnish with the green onion slices. Serve with chopsticks.

CHEFIE TIP

Leftover rice is key for fried rice. You need the rice to be dry enough to absorb the oil, making it toasty. Plan ahead, and prep everything before cooking. It goes fast. If you're impatient and want to make this now, rinse the rice until the water runs clear and cook it according to the package directions. Spread it out on a parchment paper–lined baking sheet and leave it at room temperature for several hours to dry it out.

HALIBUT WITH BRAISED CREAMED LEEKS

Cleaning the leeks three times is mandatory or you'll bite down into sand and well, that's a disaster dish! There's a restaurant that inspired me with this dish, however they don't properly clean the leeks. Clean the leeks! Everything else whips together quickly. Ask the fish monger to remove the skin or leave it on if you love crispy skin. I prefer it without the skin, paired with this sauce for a simple, clean flavor.

Wondra flour is a searing flour that dissolves easily, making a lump-free, silky smooth sauce. You can find it at most grocery stores. You can also substitute all-purpose flour.

Pair this dish with your favorite potato side; it makes for a complete and satisfying meal.

SERVES 4

4 (6-ounce [170-g]) wild halibut fillets - skin removed

3 large leeks, light green and white parts only - halved and sliced (about 3½ to 4 cups [300 to 400 g])

kosher salt

fresh finely ground black pepper

¼ cup (60 ml) avocado oil - divided

Remove the halibut from the refrigerator for 30 minutes before cooking, to remove the chill. Dry the fish really well on both sides with heavy-duty paper towels.

Place the sliced leeks into a strainer bowl of a salad spinner. Fill with cold water and agitate the leeks, shaking and rubbing between your hands to loosen any sand.

Strain and repeat three times until the water at the bottom of the bowl is clean.

Spin the leeks two times in a salad spinner and dry them really well with a clean kitchen towel. Make sure the leeks are dry before cooking.

Season the fish on both sides with ¾ teaspoon salt and ¼ teaspoon pepper.

Heat a 12-inch (30.5-cm) frying pan over medium heat for 1 minute. Add 2 tablespoons (30 ml) oil and heat the oil until it shimmers, about 20 seconds.

(continued)

HALIBUT WITH BRAISED CREAMED LEEKS

(continued)

3 tablespoons (24 g) Wondra flour

½ cup (120 ml) Homemade Chicken Stock (page 169)

½ cup (120 ml) heavy cream

2 tablespoons (28 g) cold unsalted butter

Coat the fillets in Wondra flour on both sides, shaking off any excess. Place the fillets in the frying pan, presentation side down. Sear until the fillets are golden, 2 to 2½ minutes. Don't touch it. Flip; using a fish spatula will set you up for success. Sear until the other side is golden, 2 minutes. Transfer the fillets to a plate and keep warm.

In the same pan, add the remaining 2 tablespoons (30 ml) oil and the leeks and season with ¾ teaspoon salt and ¼ teaspoon pepper. Sauté until the leeks are tender, 5 to 6 minutes, cradling the heat between medium and medium-low. Don't burn 'em.

Add the chicken stock and cook until its reduced by one-third, 30 to 45 seconds. Reduce the heat to medium-low. Pour in the cream and bring the mixture to a gentle bubble, 2 to 3 minutes, stirring occasionally.

Remove the pan from the heat. Add the cold butter and constantly stir until it is melted.

Divide the fish among four plates and spoon the creamed leeks among the halibut fillets.

FOOLPROOF PAN-SEARED SCALLOPS WITH RUSTIC MASHED POTATOES

These mashed potatoes break all my rules for the perfect mashed potatoes, which do not have lumps! But this chapter is called "Because You're Lazy," so we're making 'em the quick and lazy way (wink), plus I know you like 'em lumpy. This one's for you, still damn good and satisfying. Seafood and potatoes—the perfect combo.

SERVES 4

1½ pounds (680 g) U/16 wild sea scallops - muscles removed - divided

1½ pounds (680 g) baby red potatoes - rinsed, halved or quartered

kosher salt

12 tablespoons (168 g) unsalted butter - room temperature - divided

⅓ cup (80 ml) heavy cream

Place heavy-duty paper towels on a large platter. Add the scallops and place more heavy-duty paper towels on top of the scallops. Let them sit at room temperature to remove the chill and dry them very well to get a good sear.

Place the potatoes in a 4-quart (3.7-L) pot and fill with cold water, just covering the potatoes. Season with salt and bring to a rapid bubble over high heat.

Continue boiling until the potatoes are fork tender, about 8 minutes. Drain the potatoes and immediately return them back to the hot pot; the heat of the pot will evaporate the excess moisture in the potatoes. Don't skip this step! If you do they'll be watery. Let them sit, 5 minutes.

Meanwhile, in a 2-quart (1.9-L) sauce pot over medium-low heat, melt ½ cup (114 g) butter, continuously swirling the pan slowly. Add the heavy cream and stir until warmed through, 1 to 2 minutes. Do not let the cream come to a bubble; it'll scald it. Remove the pot from heat.

Pour the warmed, creamed butter over the potatoes and season with 1½ teaspoons (9.5 g) salt. Using a potato masher, smash the potatoes and stir well until the cream and butter are absorbed into the potatoes. Keep warm.

(continued)

FOOLPROOF PAN-SEARED SCALLOPS WITH RUSTIC MASHED POTATOES *(continued)*

fresh finely ground black pepper

4 tablespoons (60 ml) avocado oil - divided

6 fresh thyme sprigs - divided

fresh chives - thinly sliced, to garnish

Season the scallops lightly with salt and pepper on both sides.

Heat two 12-inch (30.5-cm) frying pans over medium-high heat for 1 minute. Or work with one pan at a time. You don't want to overcrowd the pan or you won't get a good sear.

Divide the oil equally between both pans, and heat it until it shimmers, 30 seconds.

Divide the scallops between both pans. Sear, don't touch it, until they are golden brown, 2 to 3 minutes. Cradle the heat between medium and medium-high. Flip the scallops. Reduce the heat to medium and sear until they are lightly golden and medium doneness, 1 minute.

Divide the remaining 4 tablespoons (56 g) butter and thyme sprigs between the pans. Swirl the pan to melt the butter and carefully tilt the pan to collect the butter in a puddle on one side. Using a tablespoon, baste the scallops with the butter until the butter is foamy, about 1 minute.

Spoon the potatoes among four plates and serve the scallops directly on top. Discard the thyme sprigs and drizzle the butter from the pan over the scallops and potatoes. Garnish with more black pepper and the chives, because you're extra fancy. Serve immediately.

CHEFIE TIP
U/16 is the size, meaning 16 scallops per pound.

PHILLY CHEESESTEAK AMERICAN WIT

I was born and raised in Delco (Delaware County, the suburbs thirteen miles outside Philly). Cheese wiz is not my food of choice by any stretch, but it's what I knew to be on a Philly cheesesteak. If you wanted your cheesesteak, Wiz Wit or Wiz Witout, go for it! I like mine American Wit. That's how you order in Philly. Wit means with or without fried onions and never finely chop the meat! I don't know whose idea that was, but it totally dries out the meat. You should also slightly gut the roll. Even though we used Amoroso rolls, the best tried and true traditional Philly rolls, the cheesesteak is the star and the roll needs to be perfectly aligned for a better ratio.

MAKES 2 SANDWICHES

4 tablespoons (60 ml) avocado, canola or peanut oil - divided

1 medium Spanish onion - diced (about 1 cup [160 g])

kosher salt

fresh finely ground black pepper

2 (¾-pound [339-g] each) rib eye steaks - excess fat trimmed, meat thinly sliced

2 fresh long Italian rolls (if living in Philly area use Amoroso's) - split and slightly gutted

8 slices American cheese

whole pickled cherry peppers, for serving

Heat a 12-inch (30.5-cm) cast-iron skillet or griddle over medium heat. When fully heated, add 1 to 2 tablespoons (15 to 30 ml) oil and the onions, and season lightly with salt and pepper. Sauté until the onions are tender yet crisp with some caramelization, 2 to 4 minutes. Transfer the onions to a bowl.

If using a 12-inch (30.5-cm) skillet, cook one steak at a time. If using a griddle, make both of them at the same time since you have more surface area for a good sear.

In the same pan, add 1 to 2 tablespoons (15 to 30 ml) oil and evenly spread out the steak slices in the pan. Don't touch the meat. Let it sear, 1 minute, grabbing some caramelization. Roughly chop the meat, using two spatulas to pull the meat apart, keeping larger bite-sized pieces. Continue to cook until the meat is no longer pink, 2 to 3 minutes. Season with salt and pepper to your liking. Return half the onions if using a 12-inch (30.5-cm) frying pan. Return all of the onions if using a griddle. Separate the steak and onions into two long bundles, if using the griddle, the same size as the length of the roll.

Add 4 slices of cheese over each steak and onions bundle. Using a spatula, lift some of the steak up and over the cheese to melt. Flip the open split side of the roll upside down and place it directly on top of the steak. Using a spatula, scoop the steak onto the roll with one hand and flip the roll over with the other hand, spreading the steak over the roll. That's how you do it, Philly style baby!

Cut each sandwich in half crosswise and serve with pickled cherry peppers on the side. Take a bite of the cheesesteak then take a bit of the pickled cherry peppers as you're eating.

PAN-FRIED CHICKEN QUESADILLAS

You can use leftover Salt and Pepper Chicken (page 68) and add it to the quesadillas, or nix the chicken and make 'em vegetarian for a quick, fresh, yet filling rockstar dinner.

SERVES 6

½ cup (120 ml) avocado oil - divided

2 medium poblano chiles - sliced

1 medium white onion - sliced

kosher salt

fresh finely ground black pepper

1 garlic clove - minced

6 (8-inch [20-cm]) House-made Flour Tortillas (page 165)

1½ cups (225 g) shredded Oaxaca cheese - divided

1 grilled Salt and Pepper Chicken breast (page 68) - thinly sliced

2 jalapeño or serrano peppers - sliced

fresh cilantro leaves

1½ cups (170 g) shredded Monterey Jack or Pepper Jack cheese - divided

FOR THE LIME CREMA

zest of ½ lime

2 tablespoons (30 ml) freshly squeezed lime juice

1 teaspoon granulated sugar

1 cup (240 ml) Mexican crema or sour cream

In a 12-inch (30.5-cm) frying pan over medium heat, heat 2 tablespoons (30 ml) oil. Add the poblanos and onions and season with 1 teaspoon salt and ¼ teaspoon pepper. Sauté until the onions are tender, 5 to 6 minutes. Add the garlic and sauté until you can smell it, about 1 minute. Remove to a bowl.

Working with 2 tortillas at a time, spread ¼ cup (23 g) Oaxaca cheese over one half of each tortilla. Add some peppers and onions, a few slices of chicken, a few slices of jalapeños, some cilantro leaves and ¼ cup (28 g) Monterey Jack or Pepper Jack cheese. Fold each tortilla over to close.

Heat 2 tablespoons (30 ml) oil in a 12-inch (30.5-cm) frying pan over medium heat. Transfer the 2 prepared tortillas into the pan, side by side. Reduce the heat to medium-low and cradle the heat between medium and medium-low while cooking. Don't burn 'em.

Cook until the quesadillas are golden, 1½ to 2 minutes. Flip. Drizzle in a little more oil, if needed and cover the pan to melt the cheese. Cook until the tortillas are golden and the cheese is melted, 1½ to 2 minutes.

Remove to a paper towel–lined plate. Season the tortillas lightly with salt. Repeat with the remaining tortillas and fillings.

FOR THE LIME CREMA: In a medium bowl, add the lime zest, lime juice and sugar, and whisk until blended. Add the crema or sour cream and whisk again until smooth.

Cut each tortilla into three triangles. Serve with the lime crema on the side for dipping.

ASIAN-STYLE GLAZED SALMON

I love how this dish tastes gourmet yet you can whip it together quickly. Serve it with cooked jasmine rice or coconut rice for a complete meal. Bird's eye chilis can be found at most Asian markets or online. You can also substitute a small Fresno or serrano chile.

SERVES 4

4 (6-ounce [170-g]) salmon fillets - skin removed

¼ cup (60 ml) hoisin

1 teaspoon finely grated fresh ginger

1 garlic clove - finely grated

2 teaspoons (10 g) granulated sugar

1 Thai bird's eye chili - minced

kosher salt

fresh finely ground black pepper

2 tablespoons (30 ml) avocado oil

toasted sesame seeds, to garnish

chopped fresh cilantro leaves, to garnish

Place the salmon on heavy-duty paper towels. Add more heavy-duty paper towels on top of the salmon and let it sit at room temperature for 25 to 30 minutes to remove the chill and absorb any excess moisture, so you get a good, golden sear.

In a small bowl, add the hoisin, ginger, *gálick*, *shugá* and chili, and stir until combined.

Season both sides of the salmon with salt and pepper.

Heat a 12-inch (30.5-cm) frying pan over medium heat for 1 minute. Add the oil and heat it until it shimmers, about 15 seconds.

Add the salmon to the pan, presentation side down (the prettier side). Sear, don't touch it, until it's golden brown, about 2 minutes. Flip and sear the other side until lightly golden and cooked to medium doneness, 1 to 2 minutes. During the last 30 seconds, turn off the heat and brush the hoison mixture over top of the salmon. Remove the salmon from the pan and divide it among four plates.

Evenly sprinkle sesame seeds over the salmon and garnish with cilantro, because you're fancy.

PRESSURE COOKER MAC AND CHEESE

Making pasta in a pressure cooker boosts a starchier pasta liquid, making this mac and cheese extra creamy and velvety. Serve with Pan-Seared New York Strip Steak (page 63), Salt and Pepper Chicken (page 68) or Spice-Rubbed Baby Back Ribs (page 37)

SERVES 4

2 tablespoons (28 g) unsalted butter - melted

1¼ teaspoons (3 g) granulated garlic - divided

½ cup (28 g) panko breadcrumbs

kosher salt

½ pound (227 g) cavatappi

1 large egg

½ cup (120 ml) half-and-half

¾ teaspoon dry mustard

1¼ cups (141 g) freshly shredded Cheddar cheese

1¼ cups (141 g) freshly shredded Monterey Jack or Pepper Jack cheese

1 tablespoon (14 g) cold unsalted butter

2 teaspoons (1.5 g) chopped fresh Italian parsley

Heat the oven to 325°F (163°C). In a small bowl, add the melted butter, ½ teaspoon granulated garlic, panko breadcrumbs and a pinch of salt, and stir to fully moisten. Spread the breadcrumb mixture out on a small rimmed baking sheet. Bake until crispy and lightly golden, 5 to 8 minutes, tossing halfway. Remove to cool.

In the pot of a 6-quart (5.5-L) pressure cooker, add the pasta, 4 cups (960 ml) water and ¾ teaspoon salt, and stir. Pressure cook on high, 3 minutes. Allow to naturally release for 3 minutes, then quick release.

Meanwhile, in a medium bowl, whisk the egg and half-and-half until combined.

Drain the pasta, reserving 1 cup (240 ml) pasta liquid. Return the pasta to the insert pot and place it back in the pressure cooker. Turn on the warm setting.

Add the egg mixture, ¾ teaspoon granulated garlic and dry mustard. Stir until slightly thickened, 2 to 5 minutes. Stir in the Cheddar cheese, Monterey Jack cheese and cold butter until melted. Thin the cheese sauce with a little pasta liquid at a time until creamy and velvety, as needed.

Transfer the mac and cheese to a medium-sized serving dish. Top with the breadcrumb mixture and garnish with parsley, because you're fancy.

COMFORT FOODS FROM AROUND THE WORLD

Asian, Mexican, French and American comfort foods you'll crave.

SPICY ORANGE CHICKEN

Get ready! 'Cause this is SO freakin' good! I added cornstarch to the coating to make it even crispier and the orange marmalade is our little secret; I discovered it more than fifteen years ago, shhh! No one needs to know; it adds sweetness and an extra boost of orange, eliminating the need for several more ingredients.

Can't find bird's eye chili? Substitute dried chile de árbol. Takara mirin can be found online, or you can substitute another sweetened sake. I've used the ones in the grocery store; it's not as good but it works. This is quick cooking, so prep all your ingredients before you start, even the cornstarch slurry and make rice to complete the meal.

SERVES 4

1 cup (240 ml) buttermilk

1½ pounds (680 g) boneless, skinless chicken thighs - cut into 1½-inch (3.8-cm) strips

¾ cup (94 g) all-purpose flour

¾ cup (96 g) cornstarch

1½ teaspoons (3.5 g) paprika

kosher salt

fresh finely ground black pepper

FOR THE ORANGE SAUCE

2 tablespoons (30 ml) avocado oil

5 garlic cloves - minced

2 to 3 bird's eye chilis - cut open lengthwise

3 tablespoons (45 ml) less-sodium soy sauce

3 tablespoons (45 ml) Takara mirin

¼ cup (60 ml) orange marmalade

peel of 1 orange

¾ cup (180 ml) freshly squeezed orange juice

In a medium, shallow bowl, add the buttermilk and toss in the chicken. Let the chicken marinate at room temperature while you prep the remaining ingredients.

In another large, shallow bowl, add the flour, cornstarch, paprika, 1¼ teaspoons (7.5 g) salt and ½ teaspoon pepper and whisk to combine.

Working in batches and in single layers, remove the chicken from the buttermilk, dripping off the excess, then dredge the chicken in the flour mixture, shaking off the excess. Set the chicken aside on a wire rack to slightly dry the coating.

TO MAKE THE ORANGE SAUCE: Heat a wok or 12-inch (30.5-cm) frying pan over medium-high heat for 30 seconds. Add 2 tablespoons (30 ml) avocado oil, the garlic and chilis and sauté until you can smell the *gálick*, about 15 seconds, cradling the heat between medium-high and medium. Don't burn the *gálick*.

In the same wok or pan, add the soy sauce, mirin, marmalade, orange peel, orange juice and ¼ teaspoon salt and stir. Bring to a bubble over medium heat. Reduce the heat and simmer to build the flavors, about 5 minutes.

(continued)

SPICY ORANGE CHICKEN *(continued)*

4 teaspoons (10 g) cornstarch

4 cups (960 ml) avocado, canola or peanut oil

3 green onions - dark green ends sliced, to garnish

In a small bowl, mix the cornstarch and 4 teaspoons (20 ml) cold water and pour it into the sauce. Bring the sauce to a bubble over medium heat until thick enough to coat the back of a spoon, 30 seconds to 1 minute. Immediately turn off the heat.

Meanwhile, in a 12-inch (30.5-cm) straight-sided sauté pan over medium heat, heat 4 cups (960 ml) oil until it shimmers and reaches 360 to 370°F (180 to 188°C), cradling the heat between medium and medium-high.

Working in three to four batches, fry the chicken pieces until golden, 2 to 3 minutes on each side. Transfer the chicken to a wire rack over a rimmed baking sheet. Season with salt immediately. Don't overcrowd the pan, or the chicken won't get nice and crispy.

Add the chicken pieces to the sauce and toss with a rubber spatula to evenly coat.

Transfer the chicken to a medium serving platter and garnish with green onions, because you're fancy.

Serve family-style with chopsticks.

CHEFIE TIP

Wet the knife and your hands when mincing garlic, so it doesn't stick to the knife or your hands.

CRISPY FRIED SHRIMP WITH SRIRACHA RÉMOULADE

Insane! Crispy exterior wrapped around sweet, meaty shrimp dipped in spicy, creamy sriracha rémoulade. Once you start eating them, you can't stop.

Buy frozen shrimp. The shrimp in the case at the grocery store has been previously frozen and you don't know how long it's been thawed. I can't tell you how many times I've gotten bad shrimp this way. Serve these crispy fried shrimp with your favorite vegetable or French fries.

SERVES 8

¾ cup (94 g) all-purpose flour

2 teaspoons (4.5 g) granulated garlic

2 teaspoons (4.5 g) onion powder

¾ teaspoon cayenne pepper

2 large eggs

¾ cup (180 ml) whole milk

1¼ cups (135 g) Italian-style breadcrumbs + more as needed

1¼ cups (70 g) panko breadcrumbs + more as needed

2 pounds (908 g) frozen large (U/21 to 25) tail-on wild shrimp - thawed, peeled, deveined

6 to 8 cups (1.4 to 1.9 L) peanut or canola oil

kosher salt

1 to 2 lemons - cut into wedges

Sriracha Rémoulade (recipe follows)

In a wide, shallow, rimmed bowl, whisk the flour, granulated garlic, onion powder and cayenne. Add the eggs. While whisking, add the milk and whisk until smooth, creating a thin batter.

In a second wide, shallow, rimmed bowl, combine the Italian and panko breadcrumbs.

Working in batches, dredge the shrimp in the batter, dripping off the excess, then dredge in the breadcrumbs, shaking off the excess. You may need to refresh the breadcrumbs if they're getting too clumpy. Set the shrimp on a parchment paper–lined baking sheet. (You can do this step several hours ahead; just cover and refrigerate the shrimp until ready to cook.)

In a heavy-bottom pot or Dutch oven, heat the oil over medium heat until it reaches 350 to 375°F (177 to 190°C). Be sure to maintain the temperature while frying.

Working in four batches, fry the shrimp until golden, 1½ to 2 minutes. Don't overcook it or it'll be tough. Transfer the shrimp to a wire cooling rack set over a rimmed baking sheet, so they don't steam and remain crispy. Immediately season the shrimp with salt. (Bring the temperature back up before adding another batch of shrimp.)

Serve lemon wedges on the side for squeezing and the sriracha rémoulade for dipping.

(continued)

CRISPY FRIED SHRIMP WITH SRIRACHA RÉMOULADE *(continued)*

SRIRACHA RÉMOULADE

I also serve this sauce with my restaurant-style crab cakes from the first cookbook, *Cooking with Shereen from Scratch: Because You Can!* It's my go-to dipping sauce for seafood.

MAKES 1¹⁄₃ CUPS (320 ML)

zest of ½ lemon

1 tablespoon (15 ml) freshly squeezed lemon juice

1 small garlic clove - finely grated

1 cup (240 ml) homemade mayonnaise (page 160)

3 sweet gherkins - minced (about ¼ cup [38 g])

1 tablespoon (10 g) capers - drained, rinsed and chopped

1 teaspoon sriracha

1 teaspoon apple cider vinegar

¼ teaspoon kosher salt

pinch fresh finely ground black pepper

In a medium bowl, add the lemon zest, lemon juice and garlic and stir to combine. The lemon mellows the *gálick*.

Add the mayonnaise, gherkins, capers, sriracha, apple cider vinegar, salt and pepper and mix well until combined. Cover and refrigerate until ready to serve. You can make this up to 1 day ahead.

SICHUAN-STYLE DAN DAN NOODLES

This Sichuan street dish is absolutely delicious! I know it's not traditional but my Udon Noodles from Scratch (page 157) delivers the same chewy textured noodle as Chinese noodles here. Or you can use store-bought Chinese noodles if you like, but if you're making the noodles, prepare them and the chili oil up to 4 days ahead. That way you can pull this dish together easily.

SERVES 6

FOR THE BEEF

1 pound (454 g) boneless beef chuck steaks - excess fat trimmed (if needed) and meat diced

3 tablespoons (45 ml) less-sodium soy sauce

2 tablespoons (30 ml) Shaoxing rice wine

2 tablespoons (12 g) finely grated ginger

4 garlic cloves - finely grated

1 tablespoon (15 ml) grapeseed oil

¾ teaspoon kosher salt

½ teaspoon freshly ground toasted Sichuan peppercorns

FOR THE CHILI OIL

½ cup (120 ml) grapeseed oil

6 garlic cloves - minced

3 to 4 green onions - thinly sliced, light and dark green parts - divided

10 to 15 fresh bird's eye chilis - stemmed and minced

1 teaspoon paprika

¾ teaspoon kosher salt

½ teaspoon freshly ground toasted Sichuan peppercorns

TO MAKE THE BEEF: In a food processor fitted with the blade attachment, add the beef and pulse chop until the beef is finely ground, 12 to 20 times. Alternately, you can use a meat grinder. Transfer the beef to a large bowl and add the soy sauce, Shaoxing rice wine, ginger and *gálick*. Mix until everything is well combined. Let the beef marinate at room temperature, 15 to 25 minutes.

TO MAKE THE CHILI OIL: In a 2-quart (1.9-L) sauce pan over low to medium-low heat, heat the oil, garlic, whites of the green onions, chilis, paprika, salt and Sichuan pepper. Sauté until the *gálick* and chilis are infused in the oil, about 10 minutes. Turn off the heat and puree the chili oil with an emulsion blender until chunky smooth. Alternatively, you can transfer the chili oil to a blender.

(continued)

SICHUAN-STYLE DAN DAN NOODLES *(continued)*

FOR THE SAUCE

¼ cup (60 ml) less-sodium soy sauce

¼ cup (60 ml) Shaoxing rice wine

1 tablespoon (15 ml) rice wine vinegar

2 teaspoons (10 ml) toasted sesame paste (such as tahini)

1 pound (454 g) Chinese noodles or Udon Noodles from Scratch (page 157)

toasted sesame oil, to garnish

toasted sesame seeds, to garnish

TO MAKE THE SAUCE: In a large bowl, add the soy sauce, Shaoxing rice wine, vinegar, sesame paste and the chili oil, and whisk vigorously until smooth. Keep warm. The sesame paste is the emulsifier and slightly thickens the sauce to help it cling to the noodles.

In a 6-quart (5.5-L) pot over high heat, bring water to a rolling bubble. Add the udon noodles and cook until tender, 10 to 12 minutes for fatter, hand rolled noodles, 5 to 6 minutes for thinner noodles. If using store-bought noodles, cook according to package directions. Drain and briefly rinse the noodles in cold water to remove some of the starch and stop the cooking, reducing the temperature but keeping them warm.

When ready to cook the beef, heat a wok or 12-inch (30.5-cm) frying pan over medium-high heat for 1 minute. Add the oil. When the oil is heated and slightly smokes, add the beef and season with salt and Sichuan pepper. Stir-fry until the beef is browned, breaking up the meat into tiny pieces and reducing the excess liquid until evaporated, about 6 to 8 minutes. Keep warm.

To serve, divide the sauce among six shallow bowls. Top with the warm Chinese noodles or Udon Noodles and the beef. Garnish with the dark green onions, a light drizzle of sesame oil and sprinkle with sesame seeds, because you're fancy!

Toss the noodles into the sauce with chopsticks as you eat.

CHEFIE TIP

Peel ginger with a teaspoon, it's easier.

PULLED PORK TACOS ROJOS

Traditionally carnitas are braised in lard, but I went for a less messy yet just as tender and flavorful version by braising the pork in its own fat with a rojo (red) sauce for deep robust *flavah*. Now, the sauce is done. You can substitute the cotija with crumbled queso fresco or shredded Monterey Jack cheese.

SERVES 8 TO 12 (2 TO 3 TACOS PER SERVING)

4 dried ancho chiles - rinsed well

2 to 3 chile de árbol - rinsed well

4 pounds (1.8 kg) bone-in pork shoulder (also called pork butt) - excess fat trimmed

kosher salt

fresh finely ground black pepper

2 tablespoons (30 ml) avocado oil (or any neutral flavored, high smoke point oil)

1 large white onion - chopped

6 garlic cloves - sliced

2 teaspoons (4 g) ground cumin

2 teaspoons (3 g) ground coriander

4 cups (960 ml) Homemade Chicken Stock (page 169)

1 bunch fresh cilantro - some stems and leaves separated - divided

Heat oven to 350°F (177°C).

Soak the chiles in boiling, hot water until softened, 30 minutes to overnight. Remove and discard the stems and seeds. Discard the water.

Heat a 6-quart (5.5-L) Dutch oven or heavy-bottomed, oven-safe pot over medium heat. Dry the pork really well with heavy-duty paper towels. Season with salt and pepper all over. Add the oil to the pot and heat, 20 seconds. Sear the pork until browned, 2 minutes on four sides, for a total of 8 minutes. Transfer the pork to a plate.

Degrease the pot, if needed, leaving 2 tablespoons (30 ml) oil in the pot. Add the onions and sauté until tender and slightly caramelized, about 5 minutes. Add the garlic and sauté until you can smell the *gálick*, 30 seconds. Reduce the heat to medium-low and add the cumin and coriander. Sauté until slightly toasted, about 20 seconds. Turn off the heat and deglaze the pot with half of the chicken stock. Transfer the mixture to a blender, scraping everything out of the pot with a rubber spatula. Add the chiles, the remaining chicken stock and a handful of cilantro stems and puree until smooth.

Pour the sauce back into the pot. Return the pork to the pot, meaty side down nestled into the sauce. Cover the pot with a tight-fitted lid and place into the oven to braise the pork until it's uber tender and easily shreds when pulled with a fork, 3 to 3½ hours.

(continued)

PULLED PORK TACOS ROJOS *(continued)*

22 to 24 (5½-inch [14-cm])
Handmade Corn Tortillas
(page 163)

TO GARNISH

1 (10-ounce [283-g]) wedge
cotija cheese - crumbed

1 to 2 large red onions - thinly
sliced into half moons

5 to 7 serrano chiles - sliced

4 limes - cut into wedges

Transfer the pork to a large plate to rest, 15 minutes. Shred the pork off the bones using two forks.

Return the shredded pork to the sauce and stir. Season with salt as needed.

Warm the corn tortillas in a cast-iron skillet, on the grill or on the burner of an open flame until slightly charred and toasted, about 15 seconds on each side. Keep warm in a tightly covered foil packet while toasting. Fill and serve immediately.

TO ASSEMBLE THE PORK TACOS: Divide the pork with the sauce among the tortillas and top with some cotija, a few de-flamed (see Chefie Tip) sliced onions, a few serranos and a good bunch of *cee-lantro* (roll the *r*), because you're fancy.

Serve lime wedges on the side for squeezing over the pork. It's a must!

CHEFIE TIPS

Toss the pork bones into a large zipper bag when cooled and freeze to make stock later when you're ready.

Crumble the cotija yourself, it's creamier and it's easier to crumble at room temperature.

To de-flame the onion, soak the sliced red onions in cold water, drain and repeat a couple times, for about 10 minutes. De-flaming the onion reduces the harsh raw onion *flavah*.

FISH TACOS WITH GREEN APPLE SLAW AND CHIPOTLE AIOLI

These are my daughter, Isabella's, absolute favorite. She was bummed they weren't in my first cookbook, so it was mandatory I added them to my second book. It's a keeper.

You will have some Chipotle Aioli left over; keep refrigerated up to three days (see Chefie Tip). Serve on burgers, sandwiches or with my Salt and Pepper Grilled Chicken (page 68) without the pesto.

SERVES 4

FOR THE GREEN APPLE SLAW

½ cup (120 ml) rice vinegar

5 tablespoons (75 g) granulated sugar

kosher salt

fresh finely ground black pepper

2 cups (140 g) thinly sliced red cabbage (about ¼ head)

1 Granny Smith apple - cored and thinly sliced into matchsticks

¾ cup (12 g) roughly chopped fresh cilantro

FOR THE CHIPOTLE AIOLI (MAKES ABOUT 1¼ CUPS [300 ML])

1 garlic clove - finely grated

2 tablespoons (30 ml) freshly squeezed lime juice

1 cup (240 ml) homemade mayonnaise (page 160)

2 chipotles in adobo - chopped, + ½ tablespoon (7.5 ml) adobo sauce

TO MAKE THE GREEN APPLE SLAW: In a large bowl, whisk the vinegar, *shugá*, 1 teaspoon salt and ¼ teaspoon pepper until combined. Add the red cabbage, apple and cilantro and evenly toss in the vinegar mixture. Cover and marinate at room temperature, 30 minutes to 2 hours, gently tossing periodically. Don't break the apple sticks.

TO MAKE THE CHIPOTLE AIOLI: In a small blender or food processor, add the garlic, lime juice and stir, 30 seconds. It mellows the *gálick*. Add the mayonnaise, chipotles, adobo sauce, ½ teaspoon salt and ⅛ teaspoon pepper and blend until smooth.

TO MAKE THE FISH: In a wide, shallow bowl, whisk the eggs. In a second wide, shallow bowl, combine the panko and Italian breadcrumbs. Dip each piece of fish (working with a couple pieces at a time) into the egg mixture, dripping off the excess. Then dredge the fish in the breadcrumbs, shaking off the excess. Transfer the fish to a plate.

Meanwhile, heat a 12-inch (30.5-cm) frying pan over medium heat. Add the oil. When the oil is heated and shimmers, add half of the breaded fish and pan-fry until golden brown, about 2 minutes on each side. Transfer the fish to a wire cooling rack and immediately season with salt. Repeat with the remaining fish.

(continued)

FISH TACOS WITH GREEN APPLE SLAW
AND CHIPOTLE AIOLI *(continued)*

FOR THE FISH

2 large eggs

½ cup (28 g) panko breadcrumbs

½ cup (54 g) Italian-style breadcrumbs

1½ pounds (680 g) skinned cod or haddock fillets - cut into 4 x ¾–inch (10 x 2–cm) pieces

1 cup (240 ml) avocado, safflower or peanut oil

10 (6-inch [15-cm]) House-made Flour Tortillas (page 165)

2 limes - cut into wedges, for serving

While frying the fish, lightly grill or toast the tortillas over an open flame until warmed through with light grill marks, 15 to 30 seconds on each side. Remove and cover in foil, so they don't dry out. Keep warm while cooking the fish.

Divide the fish among the warmed tortillas. Using tongs, divide and top the apple slaw over the fish and drizzle your desired amount of chipotle aioli over the tacos.

Serve lime wedges on the side, for squeezing over the tacos.

CHEFIE TIP

Add the chipotle aioli into a squeeze bottle for a chefie drizzled presentation, because you're fancy. You can find squeeze bottles in most grocery stores for a couple bucks.

INDIVIDUAL CHICKEN POT PIES

A top crust and bottom crust is overkill for individual-sized pot pies. I found the bottom crust absorbed the sauciness of the filling, plus the ratio was way off. The pot pie filling to puff pastry ratio is balanced perfect here. This recipe makes individually sized pot pies, so you don't have to share.

MAKES 4 INDIVIDUAL (5½- TO 6-INCH [14- TO 15-CM]) PIES

2¼ pounds (1 kg) bone-in split chicken breasts

avocado oil

kosher salt

fresh finely ground black pepper

6 tablespoons (84 g) unsalted butter

1 cup (160 g) diced Spanish onions (about 1 medium)

1 cup (90 g) diced fennel (about 1 small bulb)

1 cup (128 g) diced carrots (about 2 to 3)

5 ounces (142 g) sliced, stemmed shiitake mushrooms

2 tablespoons (4 g) fresh thyme leaves

6 small or 4 large garlic cloves - minced

6 tablespoons (48 g) all-purpose flour + more for dusting

½ cup (120 ml) good white wine

4 cups (960 ml) Homemade Chicken Stock (page 169)

¼ cup (15 g) chopped fresh Italian parsley

Heat the oven to 400°F (204°C).

Place the chicken in a 9 x 12–inch (23 x 30.5–cm) roasting pan. Lightly drizzle the skin with oil and season both sides with salt and pepper. Roast the chicken until just cooked through, 30 to 35 minutes. Remove to rest, 10 minutes. Increase the heat to 425°F (218°C).

Meanwhile, in a 6-quart (5.5-L) pot over medium heat, melt the butter. Add the onions, fennel, carrots, mushrooms and thyme. Season with 1 teaspoon salt and ¼ teaspoon pepper.

Sauté until the vegetables are tender, 7 to 9 minutes. Add the garlic and sauté until you can smell it, about 30 seconds.

Sprinkle the flour over the vegetables and stir to moisten. Deglaze with the wine. It'll immediately absorb into the flour, that's what you want. Stir, 20 seconds. Add the chicken stock. Once the stock is warmed through, taste it and season with salt if needed. Bring the mixture to a rolling bubble over medium-high heat for 1 minute to fully thicken. Reduce the heat and simmer to build flavor and create a velvety sauce, about 25 minutes, stirring periodically.

Shred the chicken off the bones into bite-sized pieces, discarding the skin.

Stir the chicken and parsley into the pot. Remove from the heat.

(continued)

INDIVIDUAL CHICKEN POT PIES *(continued)*

1 (14-ounce [392-g] package) thawed puff pastry, Dufour preferred

1 large egg - beaten

Unfold the puff pastry on a lightly floured surface. Roll out to 14 x 14 inches (35.5 x 35.5 cm). Place the pie pan rim upside down on the puff pastry. Starting at the top right corner, trace a 6¾-inch (17.5-cm) circle. Repeat with the remaining dough, making four circles. Alternatively, trim the dough according to the size of your pie pans.

Divide the chicken filling mixture among four individual 5½- to 6-inch (14- to 15-cm) pie pans.

Transfer the puff pastry circles onto a parchment paper–lined sheet pan and chill in the freezer, 10 to 12 minutes. They'll puff better.

Brush the rim of the pie plates with the beaten egg. Place the puff pastry circles on top of each pie pan, slightly pressing to adhere to the egg wash rim, otherwise they'll shrink when baking. Brush the top of the puff pastry with egg and cut three slits on top of the pastry to vent.

Place the pot pies on a rimmed baking sheet. Bake, 8 to 10 minutes to puff the pastry. Reduce the temperature to 350°F (177°C) and continue baking until golden, 25 to 30 minutes. Remove to rest, 10 minutes.

CHEFIE TIP

Toss the chicken bones in a large zipper bag and freeze to make Homemade Chicken Stock (page 169) later. You'll need way more bones than this, just keep adding them to the bag as you get them.

PORK ROAST WITH THYME ONION GRAVY

What I love about this dinner, it's simple to prepare, delicious and looks fancy when served. Beurre manié means kneaded butter; it's French! It's a quick and easy way to thicken sauces à la minute, which means quickly at the last minute.

SERVES 6 TO 8

2¼ to 2½ pounds (1 to 1.1 kg) boneless pork loin roast - tied

kosher salt

fresh finely ground black pepper

2 tablespoons (30 ml) avocado oil

BEURRE MANIÉ

2 tablespoons (28 g) unsalted butter - room temperature

2 tablespoons (16 g) all-purpose flour

1 large Spanish onion - sliced into half moons (about 1½ cups [240 g])

2 tablespoons (6 g) fresh thyme leaves + more sprigs, to garnish

¼ cup (60 ml) brandy or cognac

1½ cups (360 ml) Homemade Chicken Stock (page 169)

Remove the pork roast from the refrigerator for about 30 minutes, to remove the chill. Heat the oven to 400°F (204°C).

Dry the pork roast really well with heavy-duty paper towels. Season all over with 3 teaspoons (12 g) salt and ¾ teaspoon pepper. Heat a 12-inch (30.5-cm) oven-safe frying pan over medium heat. Add the oil. When the oil is heated and shimmers, add the pork roast and sear until golden brown, 2 minutes, on all four sides, 8 minutes total time. Place the pan directly in the oven and roast the pork until cooked to medium doneness, 20 to 24 minutes, or an internal temperature reads 130 to 133°F (54 to 56°C).

FOR THE BEURRE MANIÉ: Using a fork, knead the butter and flour in a small bowl until it forms a creamy paste. Set aside.

Remove the pork roast to rest on a plate, 8 minutes. Degrease the pan, if needed, leaving 2 tablespoons (30 ml) oil in the pan. Place the pan over medium heat. (Remember the pan is hot, so use an oven mitt while cooking.) Add the onions and thyme leaves, and season with a pinch of salt and a couple turns of pepper, from a pepper mill. Sauté until the onions are tender-crisp, about 3 minutes. Reduce the heat to low and continue sautéing the onions until caramelized, about 4 minutes.

Increase the heat to medium. Deglaze with cognac or brandy, being careful of flare-ups and cook until reduced by half, about 20 seconds. Add the chicken stock and continue to cook until reduced by half, 2 to 3 minutes. If the chicken stock is cold, increase the heat a little to get it going, then reduce to medium. Remove the pan from the heat. Whisk in the beurre manié until smooth and velvety. Taste it and season to taste, if needed.

Slice the pork roast into ½-inch (1-cm) slices. Spoon the thyme onion gravy over a medium platter and arrange the sliced pork on top. Garnish with thyme sprigs. Now, you're super fancy!

POT ROAST WITH GARLICKY MUSHROOMS AND FENNEL GRAVY

Choose the flat chuck roast, not the rump, that way it stays fully submerged in the broth while cooking for an uber tender, succulent roast. If you want the gravy a little thicker, see my Chefie Tip for how to make a beurre manié.

SERVES 6 TO 8

3-pound (1.4-kg) boneless beef chuck roast - dried well

kosher salt

fresh finely ground black pepper

2 tablespoons (30 ml) avocado oil

1 small bulb fennel - cored, chopped into large pieces

1 medium yellow onion - chopped into large pieces

3 garlic cloves - smashed

3 tablespoons (45 ml) Worcestershire sauce

1 small bundle fresh thyme (wrapped in butcher's twine) + 2 tablespoons (4 g) fresh thyme leaves - divided

Heat the oven to 325°F (163°C).

Remove the roast from the refrigerator for about 30 minutes, to remove the chill. Season the roast all over with salt and pepper.

In a 5½-quart (5-L) Dutch oven over medium heat, heat the oil. When the oil is heated, add the roast and sear until lightly golden, 2 to 3 minutes on each side. Transfer the roast to a plate.

Degrease the pot, if needed, leaving 2 to 3 tablespoons (30 to 45 ml) oil in the pot. Add the fennel and onions, and sauté until the vegetables are slightly tender and caramelized, 3 to 4 minutes. Add the smashed garlic cloves and sauté until you can smell the *gálick*, about 1 minute.

Deglaze the pot with 1 cup (240 ml) water and stir to scrape up the fond (brown bits) from the bottom of the pot. Stir in the Worcestershire and thyme bundle. Return the roast to the pot, nestling it under the vegetables. Add another 2 to 3 cups (480 to 720 ml) water to almost cover the roast. Cover the pot with a tight-fitted lid and place it in the oven. Braise until the meat is uber tender and easily shredded with two forks, 3 to 3½ hours.

(continued)

POT ROAST WITH GARLICKY MUSHROOMS AND FENNEL GRAVY *(continued)*

6 tablespoons (84 g) cold unsalted butter - divided

1 pound (454 g) cremini or white button mushrooms - wiped clean and halved or quartered

4 garlic cloves - minced

2 to 3 tablespoons (8 to 11 g) chopped fresh Italian parsley, to garnish

For the mushrooms, in a 12-inch (30.5-cm) frying pan, melt 4 tablespoons (56 g) of the butter over medium heat. Add the mushrooms, 2 tablespoons (4 g) thyme leaves, 1 teaspoon salt and ¼ teaspoon pepper. Sauté the mushrooms until golden, 6 to 7 minutes. Add the minced garlic and sauté until you can smell it, about 1 minute.

Transfer the roast to a platter to rest, 8 to 10 minutes. Remove and discard the thyme bundle. Using an immersion blender or a standing blender, puree the vegetables with the broth until smooth. If using a blender, return the gravy to the pot. Heat the pot over low heat. Add the beurre manié (see Chefie Tip), if using and simmer until slightly thickened, 2 to 4 minutes. If the gravy is thick enough, nix the beurre manié and finish only with 2 tablespoons (28 g) cold butter and stir vigorously until melted, off the heat. Don't break the gravy (see Chefie Tip on page 25). Season to taste.

Shred or slice the roast into ½-inch- (1-cm-) thick slices arranged on a medium platter. Drizzle a little gravy over the roast. Top with the mushrooms and garnish with freshly cracked black pepper and parsley, because you're fancy. Serve remaining gravy on the side to pass around the table.

CHEFIE TIP

Beurre manié will make your gravy a tad thicker. Knead equal parts cold butter and flour (about 2 tablespoons each [28 g] and [16 g]) together, creating a paste and whisk it into the gravy at the end, after the puree.

TOMATO BASIL SOUP WITH GRILLED CHEESE CROUTONS

No canned soup! You're better than that. When I stress to eliminate the tomato puree from the San Marzanos, I have good reason and explain why in the headnote on page 10. This soup is incredibly delicious!

I portioned a full-sized bowl and enough grilled cheese croutons, almost equaling one sandwich, to make a complete dinner.

SERVES 4 TO 5

4 tablespoons (56 g) unsalted butter

1 large onion - diced (about 1½ cups [240 g])

kosher salt

fresh finely ground black pepper

4 garlic cloves - minced

2 (28-ounce [794-g]) jars canned fresh tomatoes (page 140) or 2 cans whole peeled San Marzano tomatoes

3 cups (720 ml) Homemade Chicken Stock (page 169)

½ cup (12 g) packed fresh basil leaves

½ cup (120 ml) heavy cream

Heat the oven to 400°F (204°C).

Melt butter in a 6-quart (5.5-L) pot over medium heat. Add the onions and season with ½ teaspoon salt and ¼ teaspoon pepper. Sauté until the onions are tender, 2 to 3 minutes. Add the garlic and sauté until you can smell it, about 1 minute.

Meanwhile, in a medium bowl, crush the tomatoes with clean hands. If using San Marzanos, drain the tomatoes, place them in a medium bowl and crush them with clean hands. Don't be a wimp! Fill the cans one-quarter of the way with cold water and swirl to release the tomato juice from the walls of the cans. Add the tomato water to the tomatoes.

In the pot with the onions, add the chicken stock, hand-crushed tomatoes and basil and season with 2 teaspoons (12 g) salt and 1 teaspoon pepper. Stir. Bring to a gentle bubble over medium-high heat, then reduce the heat to medium-low and continue to cook until the flavors build and the soup reduces slightly, 40 to 45 minutes, stirring periodically.

Working in two batches, transfer the tomato soup mixture into a blender. (Hold a kitchen towel over the lid of the blender while pureeing or the pressure from the heat will blow off the lid.) Puree until smooth. Return the soup to the pot. Stir in the heavy cream and heat over medium-low until warmed through, about 5 minutes.

(continued)

TOMATO BASIL SOUP WITH GRILLED CHEESE CROUTONS *(continued)*

FOR THE GRILLED CHEESE CROUTONS

¾ cup (170 g) unsalted butter - room temperature

8 (½-inch- [1-cm-] thick) bread slices (page 146 or 149)

1 large garlic clove

2 cups (226 g) shredded white Cheddar cheese

FOR THE GRILLED CHEESE CROUTONS: Spread the butter over both sides of the bread slices and place them on a rimmed baking sheet.

Evenly season one side of the bread slices with a little salt and pepper.

Bake until golden and toasted, 10 to 12 minutes, flipping halfway through the baking time. Remove from the oven. While still hot, rub the garlic clove on one side of the toasts.

Reduce the oven temperature to 375°F (190°C). Set aside 4 toasts.

Line the baking sheet with parchment paper and place 4 toasts on the baking sheet. Evenly mound the cheese over the toast. Return to the oven, open faced, and bake until the cheese is melted, 3 to 5 minutes. Remove from the oven and immediately top each cheese toast with the reserved toasted slices, making sandwiches. Let set a couple minutes to melt together, then cut into ½-inch (1-cm) cubes.

Divide the soup among four to five bowls. Garnish with freshly cracked black pepper and a few grilled cheese croutons. Serve the remaining croutons on the side to add to the soup as you eat.

CHEFIE TIP

If you're using larger leftover Peasant Bread (page 149) slices, cut 1 slice in half, counting it as 2 slices, since they're bigger.

SOUPE À L'OIGNON GRATINÉE (FRENCH ONION SOUP)

Sweet onions, although they seem like a good idea for this preparation, cannot withstand the long cooking time because of their higher sugar content. When cooked for a long period of time, they become mushy and mealy. Spanish onions are basically yellow onions, so you can use those, too.

MAKES 8 (12- TO 14-OUNCE [336- TO 392-G]) CROCKS

½ cup (114 g) unsalted butter

5 to 6 extra large Spanish onions (about 4 pounds [1.8 kg]) - sliced into half moons

¼ cup (10 g) fresh thyme leaves

kosher salt

fresh finely ground black pepper

½ cup (120 ml) cognac

8 cups (1.9 L) Homemade Beef Stock (page 170)

3 tablespoons (45 ml) Worcestershire sauce

8 cups (890 g) freshly shredded Gruyère cheese (from 2- to 2½-pound [908-g to 1.1-kg] wedges)

FOR THE GARLIC TOAST

½ day old French baguette - cut into 16 (½- to ⅝-inch [1- to 1.4-cm]) slices

5 tablespoons (70 g) unsalted butter

kosher salt

fresh finely ground black pepper

1 garlic clove

Divide and melt the butter among 2 (6-quart [5.5-L]) heavy-bottomed pots or 1 (6-quart [5.5-L]) heavy-bottomed pot and 1 (12-inch [30.5-cm]) sauté pan over medium heat. Divide the onions, thyme, 2½ teaspoons (15 g) salt and 1 teaspoon pepper among each pot. (If you add all of the onions to one pot, they will steam and not get beautifully caramelized.) Toss the onions to evenly coat in the butter and salt and pepper, 1 to 2 minutes. Sauté until deeply golden and caramelized, 30 to 40 minutes, tossing periodically with a rubber spatula. After 10 minutes of cooking, reduce the heat between medium-low to low. Don't let the onions stick and burn.

Heat the oven to 375°F (190°C). Divide and deglaze each pot with cognac and reduce by half, about 20 seconds. Transfer the onions, using a rubber spatula, into one 6-quart (5.5-L) pot. Stir in the beef stock and Worcestershire and bring to a gentle bubble over medium-high heat, then reduce to simmer, 10 to 15 minutes. Taste it and season with salt and pepper, if needed.

FOR THE GARLIC TOAST: Smear one side of the bread slices with butter and place them on a rimmed baking sheet. Lightly season with salt and pepper. Bake until lightly golden and toasted, 12 to 14 minutes, flipping halfway through baking. Remove the toasts and immediately rub the garlic clove over the buttered side of the hot toast. Adjust the oven rack to the upper second level. Heat to broil.

Ladle the soup among eight (12- to 14-ounce [336- to 392-g]) heat-safe soup bowls, filling two-thirds of the way. Place half of the bowls on a foil-lined rimmed baking sheet. Add ½ cup (50 g) cheese on top of each soup bowl. Top each with 2 garlic toasts and add another ½ cup (50 g) cheese on top of the toasts, so the toasts don't sink to the bottom. Place the bowls under the broiler until the cheese is melted and bubbly, 2 to 3 minutes. Remove and carefully place the hot bowls on heat-safe plates. Repeat with the remaining crocks of soup.

CLASSIC CHICKEN NOODLE SOUP

This is the ultimate comfort food. The flavors are simple and clean and it nourishes the heart and soul. Serve the soup with freshly grated Parmigiano-Reggiano over top and freshly baked, crusty bread (page 149), smeared with buttah on the side for dipping.

MAKES 16 CUPS (3.8 L); SERVES 6 TO 8

1 (4- to 4½-pound [1.8- to 2-kg]) whole chicken - giblets removed, legs tied together

8 large carrots - trimmed and peeled, 4 chopped and 4 sliced (about 2 cups [256 g]) - divided

5 celery stalks - large chop, leaves reserved - divided

1 large Spanish onion - quartered

5 fresh or 2 dry bay leaves

½ tablespoon (3.5 g) black peppercorns

1 small bunch fresh thyme or dill

1 small bunch fresh Italian parsley

kosher salt

6 ounces (170 g) dried or 12 ounces (340 g) fresh homemade egg noodles (page 153)

¼ cup (60 ml) freshly squeezed lemon juice

In an 8-quart (7.5-L) pot, add the chicken, 4 chopped carrots, chopped celery stalks, onion, bay leaves, peppercorns, thyme and parsley. Fill with 14 to 16 cups (3.3 to 3.8 L) cold water, leaving about 2 inches (5 cm) from the top of the pot. Bring to a bubble over high heat, then reduce to simmer, cover and cook until the chicken is just cooked though, 45 minutes to 1 hour.

Remove the chicken and let it cool enough to handle. Discard the skin and shred the meat off the bones. Place the chicken in a large bowl and cover to keep it moist. Refrigerate the chicken while cooking the stock.

Return the bones back to the pot and cover. Simmer 3 hours.

Strain the stock into a strainer placed over a large heat-safe bowl. Push down on the solids; discarding the bones and the solids. Strain the stock again through a fine-mesh strainer over a large heat-safe bowl. Return the stock back to the pot. Season with 2 tablespoons (34 g) salt.

Bring the stock to a rapid bubble over high heat. Add the sliced carrots and celery leaves and cook until tender-crisp, 4 minutes. Add the noodles and cook, 6 minutes for dried or 2 to 3 minutes for fresh. Turn off the heat and let it cool a bit, it's too hot to eat right now. Stir in the shredded chicken and lemon juice before serving. Taste it and season with salt, if needed.

CHEFIE TIP

Ladle leftover cooled chicken noodle soup in clear, freezer-safe quart-sized containers with tight-fitted lids. Refrigerate, up to 4 days, or freeze, up to 3 months.

PAN-ROASTED CHICKEN THIGHS WITH BUTTER BEANS

My recipe teaches you how to crisp chicken skin perfectly. There's a little technique to it and it builds great flavor for this easy skillet rockstar dinner.

SERVES 2 TO 3

4 large bone-in, skin-on chicken thighs (1½ to 1¾ pounds [680 to 795 g])

kosher salt

fresh finely ground black pepper

2 tablespoons (30 ml) avocado oil

1 medium Spanish onion - sliced

1½ tablespoons (3 g) fresh thyme leaves

1 teaspoon fennel seeds - crushed

3 garlic cloves - minced

2 tablespoons (30 ml) red wine vinegar

¾ cup (180 ml) Homemade Chicken Stock (page 169)

1 (15.5-ounce [439-g]) can butter beans - drained, rinsed

1 small bunch Tuscan kale (4 to 5 ounces [113 to 142 g]) - stemmed and leaves torn

2 tablespoons (28 g) cold unsalted butter

Heat the oven to 400°F (204°C). Dry the chicken thighs really well with heavy-duty paper towels. Season the chicken with 1¼ teaspoons (7.5 g) salt and ½ teaspoon pepper on both sides. Set aside.

Heat a 12-inch (30.5-cm) oven-safe sauté pan over medium-low heat for 2 minutes. Add the oil. When the oil is heated and shimmers, about 30 seconds, add the chicken, skin side down. Cook, rendering the fat from the chicken, about 5 minutes (slowly rendering the fat cooks the skin from the inside first, giving you even, crispy skin throughout). Increase the heat to medium and pan-fry the chicken until the skin is golden brown, 4 to 5 minutes. Rotate (do not flip) halfway through cooking. Flip the chicken over and sear, 30 seconds. Transfer the chicken to a plate. Carefully degrease the pan, leaving 2 tablespoons (30 ml) oil in the pan. Return the skillet to medium heat. Add the onions, thyme and fennel seeds. Sauté until the onions are tender-crisp, about 2 to 3 minutes. Add the garlic and sauté until you can smell it, about 45 seconds.

Deglaze with vinegar and reduce by two-thirds, about 10 seconds, while constantly swirling the pan. Add the chicken stock and butter beans to the pan. Season with ¾ teaspoon salt and ¼ teaspoon pepper. Stir well. Bring the stock to a gentle simmer over medium heat. Return the chicken to the pan, skin side up, nestled among the bean mixture. Remove the pan from the heat and place the skillet in the oven to roast the chicken until it's cooked through and juicy, 12 to 15 minutes. Remove the skillet and return it to the stove.

Transfer the chicken to a plate. Heat the skillet over medium-low and toss in the kale. Cook until the kale is slightly wilted, 1 to 2 minutes. Taste it and season with salt and pepper, if needed. Remove the pan from the heat and stir the butter into the kale bean mixture until melted. Don't break the sauce (see Chefie Tip on page 25). Transfer the kale bean mixture to a medium serving platter and place the chicken, skin side up on top.

AFTER DINNER *SHUGÁ*

Five of my favorite desserts to complete a rockstar dinner.

ICED LEMON LOAF

My riff on Starbucks's popular iced lemon loaf went viral on TikTok with more than 10.8 million views and 1.9 million likes to date. Save your money, make your own. Please use the metric *shugá* and flour measurements in this recipe for baking success.

MAKES 1 LOAF

1¼ cups (260 g) granulated sugar

zest of 1 lemon - finely grated (about 2 tablespoons [12 g])

¼ cup (60 ml) freshly squeezed lemon juice

3 large eggs

⅔ cup (160 ml) whole buttermilk

½ cup (120 ml) vegetable or canola oil

2 cups (276 g) unbleached all-purpose flour

2 teaspoons (9 g) baking powder

½ teaspoon baking soda

¾ teaspoon kosher salt

FOR THE LEMON GLAZE

1⅔ cups (200 g) confectioners' sugar

3 tablespoons (45 ml) freshly squeezed lemon juice

Heat the oven to 350°F (177°C).

In the bowl of a stand mixer fitted with the whisk attachment, add the *shugá*, lemon zest, lemon juice, eggs, buttermilk and oil, and mix until combined.

In a large bowl, whisk the flour, baking powder, baking soda and salt until combined. Pour the flour mixture onto the center of an 18-inch- (46-cm-) long piece of parchment or wax paper in a straight line. With the stand mixer on low speed, carefully pick up the paper and slowly funnel the flour into the bowl of the stand mixer. This way the flour won't waft all over you and make a mess. Gradually increase the speed to medium, scraping down the sides and under the bottom of the bowl's dimple as needed until blended. Don't overmix!

Spray a 9 x 5–inch (23 x 13–cm) loaf pan with baking spray. Line the pan with an 11 x 7½–inch (28 x 19–cm) parchment paper sling. It'll help lift it out of the pan after baking, in case the loaf sticks to the pan. Pour the batter evenly into the prepared loaf pan. Gently tap the bottom of the pan on a towel (protecting the glass loaf pan, if using) to prevent air pockets. Bake until the top is set and a long wooden skewer comes out clean, 40 to 45 minutes.

FOR THE LEMON GLAZE: In a medium bowl, whisk the confectioners' *shugá* and lemon juice until smooth. Cover with plastic wrap.

Remove the lemon loaf from the oven and let set to rest, 5 to 8 minutes. Using a butter knife, loosen the ends and lift the lemon loaf up and out of the pan with the parchment paper sling. Place the loaf on a wire rack to cool completely. Re-whisk the glaze until smooth and drizzle over the cooled lemon loaf. Let it set to harden the glaze, 20 to 30 minutes. Slice the loaf into ½-inch (1-cm) slices.

FOOLPROOF CREAMY CHEESECAKE

This is a make ahead dessert. There's almost two hours baking time, two hours resting time and four hours (or overnight) refrigeration time, but it's worth every minute of the wait. Plan ahead. I freakin' love this cheesecake!

SERVES 10

FOR THE CRUST

1½ cups (180 g) graham cracker crumbs

3 tablespoons (45 g) granulated sugar

¼ teaspoon ground cinnamon

4 tablespoons (56 g) unsalted butter - melted

FOR THE CHEESECAKE FILLING

4 (8-ounce [226-g]) packages cream cheese - room temperature

1¼ cups (150 g) granulated sugar

1 cup (240 ml) sour cream - room temperature

2 teaspoons (10 ml) pure vanilla extract

4 large eggs - room temperature

TO GARNISH

¾ pound (340 g) fresh strawberries - hulled and halved or quartered

½ pint (150 g) fresh blueberries

Heat the oven to 325°F (163°C).

FOR THE CRUST: In a large bowl, add the graham crackers, *shugá*, cinnamon and butter, and mix with a fork until well combined and moistened. Lightly spray a 9-inch (23-cm) springform pan with nonstick cooking spray. Add the graham cracker mixture to the pan, pressing evenly and firmly on the bottom (using a ramekin or the bottom of a glass), forming the crust. Bake until the crust is lightly golden, about 8 minutes. Remove to cool.

Lower the heat to 225°F (107°C). Open the oven door to help lower the internal temperature for a few minutes. Check the temperature with an oven thermometer and once is reaches 225°F (107°C), close the door. (This is a very important step that ensures the oven is at the proper temperature, so the cheesecake does not crack.)

FOR THE CHEESECAKE FILLING: In the bowl of a stand mixer fitted with the whisk attachment, mix the cream cheese, *shugá*, sour cream and vanilla extract until smooth. Add the eggs, one at a time, and continue mixing until blended, scraping down the sides and bottom cavity of the bowl.

Pour the cream cheese mixture into the cooled graham cracker crust. Bake until the filling is set with a slight wiggle in the center, 1 hour 45 minutes. Turn off the oven and leave the oven door ajar to vent, letting the cheesecake set inside for 15 minutes. (This step prepares the cheesecake for room temperature, so it doesn't crack.)

Transfer the cheesecake to a cooling rack to fully cool at room temperature, about 2 hours. Cover the springform pan with a clean kitchen towel, not touching the cake but tightly fitted under the pan and refrigerate until completely set, 4 hours to overnight. Run a butter knife around the perimeter of the springform pan and unclip the side wall. Transfer the cheesecake to a large plate. Arrange the berries on top of the cheesecake. Serve within a couple hours.

PUMPKIN PIE FROM SCRATCH

Creamy and perfectly, sweetly spiced, this recipe is your guide to the perfect pumpkin pie. To manage this recipe without feeling overwhelmed, roast and puree the pumpkin up to a few days ahead (keep refrigerated) and make the pie dough the day before and refrigerate. After preparing the pumpkin filling, you will have some roasted pumpkin puree leftover. Store it in a container with a tight-fitting lid and refrigerate, up to one week. It's great for making pancakes, muffins, soup or ravioli, just to name a few ideas.

MAKES 1 (9-INCH [23-CM]) PIE

FOR THE PUMPKIN PUREE

1 (3-pound [1.3-kg]) sugar or pie pumpkin

1 tablespoon (15 ml) avocado oil

FOR THE PIE CRUST

1½ cups (197 grams) all-purpose flour + more for dusting

½ teaspoon kosher salt

4 tablespoons (56 g) cold unsalted butter - small dice

4 tablespoons (54 g) cold vegetable shortening - small dice

3 to 4 tablespoons (45 to 60 ml) ice-cold water

Heat the oven to 375°F (190°C).

FOR THE PUMPKIN PUREE: Cut a circle around the stem of the pumpkin and remove. Cut the pumpkin in half lengthwise (top to bottom). Remove and discard the seeds and scrape out the guts and strings using a tablespoon. Brush the flesh with oil. Place the pumpkin halves cut side down on a parchment paper–lined rimmed baking sheet. Bake until the pumpkin is tender when pierced with a paring knife, 45 to 50 minutes. Remove to cool. Peel back, remove and discard the skin. It should remove easily. Once the pumpkin is cooled, place it in a food processor fitted with the steel blade attachment and puree until silky smooth, stopping the food processor and scraping down the pumpkin puree with a rubber spatula, as needed. Clean and dry the food processor really well.

FOR THE PIE CRUST: In a food processor fitted with the steel blade attachment, add 1½ cups (197 g) flour and salt. Pulse a few times to combine. Add the cold butter and shortening and pulse several times until the mixture forms a sandy texture. Slowly pour the ice-cold water through the feed tube while running the processor until the mixture forms a ball. (This happens quick, about 16 seconds.) Immediately stop adding the water when the mixture begins to form the ball. Transfer the dough to a lightly floured surface and form the dough into a 6-inch (15-cm) disk. Wrap the dough disk in plastic wrap and refrigerate until chilled, 1 hour to overnight.

(continued)

PUMPKIN PIE FROM SCRATCH *(continued)*

FOR THE PUMPKIN FILLING

¾ cup (150 g) granulated sugar

1½ teaspoons (4 g) ground cinnamon

¾ teaspoon ground ginger

¾ teaspoon ground allspice

½ teaspoon freshly grated nutmeg

½ teaspoon kosher salt

¼ teaspoon ground cloves

1 cup (240 ml) heavy cream - room temperature

3 large eggs - room temperature

Remove the dough from the refrigerator and transfer it to a lightly floured surface. Roll the dough into a 12-inch (30.5-cm) circle. Using a pizza cutter, trim any frayed edges. Ease the dough into a 9-inch (23-cm) pie plate. Fold the overhanging dough under itself around the perimeter. Using two fingers, pinch a zigzag shape to form the crust edges. Place the dough back into the refrigerator to chill, 10 minutes. (If using a glass pie plate, do not chill any longer because the heat of the oven may crack it [see Chefie Tip].)

Line the pie dough with parchment paper, covering up the sides of the dough and fill with pie weights or dried beans. Bake, 15 minutes. Remove the parchment paper and pie weights or dried beans. Reduce the oven temperature to 350°F (177°C), leaving the oven door open until the oven temperature reads 350°F (177°C). Continue baking the pie crust to set the bottom crust with no browning, 6 to 8 minutes. Transfer the pie crust to a wire cooling rack to cool.

FOR THE PUMPKIN FILLING: in a large bowl, whisk the *shugá*, cinnamon, ginger, allspice, nutmeg, salt and cloves until well blended. Add the cream and eggs. Whisk until the eggs are well combined. Add 2 cups (480 ml) of the freshly pureed roasted pumpkin and whisk until smooth. Pour the pumpkin filling into the cooled pie crust.

Bake until the filling is puffed but slightly wiggly in the center when shaken, about 50 to 55 minutes. Transfer to a wire cooling rack to cool.

CHEFIE TIPS

A glass Pyrex pie plate is not fancy but makes a crack free, foolproof pie. I've found metal heats hotter, creating cracks in the filling; if using metal, reduce the oven temp by 25°F.

You can make the pie one day ahead and keep it in a cool, dry place. No need to refrigerate.

HOLIDAY EGG NOG

My son, Costas, loves egg nog. He drinks it like it's a regular glass of milk. Lots of it. When I developed this recipe for Incredible Egg, I honestly didn't expect it to be this good. I was blown away! I never really cared for egg nog from the market, but this version is freaking' amazing! Don't think about it, just make it!

MAKES ABOUT 6 TO 7 CUPS (1.4 TO 1.6 L)

6 large eggs - whites and yolks separated

¾ cup (150 g) granulated sugar - divided

3 cups (720 ml) whole milk

1 cup (240 ml) heavy cream

1½ teaspoon (3.5 g) freshly grated nutmeg

1 teaspoon ground cinnamon + more to garnish

½ teaspoon kosher salt

⅛ teaspoon ground cloves

In the bowl of a stand mixer fitted with the whisk attachment, add the egg yolks. Whisk on high speed while slowly streaming in ½ cup (100 g) *shugá* until pale yellow and fluffy, about 2 minutes.

In a 2½-quart (2.3-L) pot over medium-low heat, whisk the milk, heavy cream, nutmeg, cinnamon, salt and cloves until warmed but not hot, 130 to 135°F (54 to 57°C), 3 to 5 minutes.

With the stand mixer on medium speed, slowly drizzle two to three ladles of the warmed milk into the egg yolks, then pour the tempered eggs into the pot with the milk mixture. Cradle the heat between medium to medium-low and cook, stirring constantly with a rubber spatula until the egg nog is slightly thickened and coats the back of a spoon, about 15 minutes, reaching 180 to 182°F (82 to 83°C). Don't walk away or the eggs could scramble! You'll achieve 180°F (82°C) much sooner than 15 minutes but continue stirring the full time for an enriched, creamy texture.

Remove from the heat and strain through a fine-mesh strainer over a large bowl, discarding any solids.

Clean and dry the stand mixer bowl and whisk. Add the egg whites to the stand mixer and whisk at medium to medium-low speed until frothy, about 1 minute. While whisking, slowly stream in the remaining ¼ cup (50 g) *shugá* and continue whisking until medium peaks, about 1 minute.

(continued)

HOLIDAY EGG NOG *(continued)*

¼ cup (60 ml) dark rum (optional)

2 teaspoons (10 ml) pure vanilla extract

Working a little at a time, add the meringue into the hot egg nog and whisk until smooth. Stir in the rum, if using, and vanilla. Cool completely.

Transfer the egg nog to a glass container with a tight-fitted lid.

Refrigerate until well chilled, 2 to 3 hours, shaking periodically as it's chilling. It'll separate, *donta* you worry. Let it set overnight for best *flavah*.

Shake vigorously and pour into rocks glasses. Add more rum and serve over ice, if desired. Garnish with a sprinkle of cinnamon, because you're fancy.

Store the egg nog in the refrigerator, up to 3 days.

CHEFIE TIP

You can also drizzle the egg nog over vanilla ice cream, add it to coffee or use it to make bread pudding.

HOMEMADE CANNOLI

Fun fact: I used to work at Carlo's Bake Shop in Hoboken, New Jersey, for Cake Boss, Buddy Valastro. Each day, I'd enter through the back door and snag a freshly piped cannoli off the speed rack as I headed up the stairs to the cake decorating room, where I worked. With each bite I moaned. Yes, they're that good. Don't get excited, I never made the cannoli at the bakery, so I have no clue what the recipe is. However, I created my version with inspiration from the flavors and texture that made me moan. I'm proud to say, these are MacDaddy! One important tip I've learned from Buddy's cannoli: Don't be stingy with the filling.

Don't use the ricotta cheese from the dairy aisle. Instead, go for homemade or hand-dipped ricotta from the cheese section of some grocery stores or Italian markets. I've found BelGioioso brand is a creamy and delicious ricotta as well. And don't choose a cheap chocolate. You deserve the best! It makes a difference.

Special equipment: 4¼-inch (10.7-cm) ring mold, pasta roller, cannoli tube molds, deep-fry thermometer.

MAKES 9 TO 11 CANNOLI

FOR THE FILLING

32 ounces (896 g) fresh whole-milk ricotta cheese

2 cups (240 g) confectioners' sugar + more to garnish

1¼ teaspoon (1.5 g) ground cinnamon

¾ teaspoon pure vanilla extract

¾ cup (130 g) good-quality, extra-dark chocolate chips (Guittard recommended) - chopped (see Chefie Tip)

FOR THE FILLING: Double line a strainer with cheesecloth and place a large bowl under the strainer. Make sure the bowl is high enough so the strainer doesn't touch the bottom of the bowl. Add the ricotta in the cheesecloth and place a piece of plastic wrap on top of the ricotta. Add a small plate directly on top. Place something heavy, like a 24-fluid-ounce (710-ml) juice bottle or many cans, on top to weigh it down, pressing the milk liquid through the strainer. The liquid is the enemy to the cannoli, get rid of it! This step is crucial for a perfectly thick and creamy filling. Refrigerate the ricotta while it's straining for several hours to overnight.

Discard the excess milk liquid from the bowl and place the ricotta into a stand mixture fitted with the whisk attachment. Add the confectioners' *shugá*, cinnamon and vanilla. Mix on low speed until smooth but not whipped, about 1 minute. Stir in the chocolate pieces until combined.

(continued)

HOMEMADE CANNOLI *(continued)*

FOR THE CANNOLI SHELLS

1 cup (140 g) Tipo "00" extra-fine unbleached Italian flour

1 tablespoon (15 g) granulated sugar

¼ teaspoon ground cinnamon

¼ teaspoon kosher salt

2 tablespoons (26 g) chilled vegetable shortening

1 large egg - yolk and white separated

4 tablespoons (45 ml) marsala wine

8 cups (1.9 L) canola or peanut oil

Transfer the mixture to a large piping bag with no tip (don't over fill it) and refrigerate to chill and firm up, about 30 minutes to overnight.

FOR THE CANNOLI SHELLS: In the bowl of a stand mixer, stir the flour, granulated *shugá*, cinnamon and salt by hand using the dough hook attachment. Rub the shortening into the flour between your hands creating tiny, pea-sized crumbles.

Fit the mixer with the dough hook and on low speed, add the egg yolk (set aside the white). Slowly pour in the marsala until the flour mixture is partially moistened, pushing down the flour with a rubber spatula to coax the flour to combine. When the mixture begins pulling together with a few dry crumbles in the bottom of the bowl, increase the speed to medium-low, kneading the dough. After 1 to 2 minutes, the dough should form a ball, naturally pulling away from the sides of the bowl. It should not stick to the bowl. If it's sticking, lightly dust with flour. If it's too dry, add a couple splashes of water; a little goes a long way.

Continue kneading the dough in the stand mixer until smooth, 5 to 6 minutes. Divide the dough in half. Flatten each half into a disk and tightly wrap with plastic wrap.

Note: This dough makes about 18 to 22 shells, but we only need the 1 disk for this recipe. Place the other plastic-wrapped disk in a freezer-safe zipper bag and freeze for up to 3 months, for another use.

Let the 1 dough disk that we're working with rest, 1 hour at room temperature or overnight in the refrigerator. Before working with the dough, remove it to room temperature 30 minutes prior, to remove the chill.

Heat the oil in a heavy bottom 6-quart (5.5-L) pot to 360 to 370°F (180 to 188°C), using a deep-fry thermometer. Adjust the heat between medium to medium-low to maintain the temperature.

Roll out the dough with a pasta roller, just like you would pasta (see directions on page 156), rolling it out to #6 on speed #6 or #8 to about $\frac{1}{16}$-inch (1.5-mm) thick, dusting with flour, as needed. If you are rolling the dough out with a rolling pin, have both dough disks on hand, working with half of the dough at a time in case you need the extra, leaving room for errors.

Using a 4¼-inch (10.7-cm) ring mold or a bowl of the same size, trace the shape onto the dough. Cut 5 to 6 circles from the dough sheet and place them onto a parchment paper–lined baking sheet. Cover the dough circles with a slightly damp, clean kitchen towel so they don't dry out.

Knead the scraps together by hand. Flatten and re-roll the dough back through the pasta roller, repeating the process. Cut 3 to 4 more circles from the small dough sheet and place the circles on the parchment paper, keeping them covered as you continue working. Re-roll the remaining scraps to get 1 to 2 more circles. You should have 9 to 11 circles at this point.

Working 3 to 4 cannoli at a time, tightly wrap the dough circles around the cannoli molds and moisten around the perimeter with warm water or brush with the egg white where it overlaps the dough, gently press to seal closed.

Place the cannoli shells in the hot oil and gently press and hold them down in the oil, using a wok strainer, so they don't bobble. Fry until golden, about 2 minutes. Transfer the shells to cool on a wire cooling rack over a rimmed baking sheet. Using two tongs, carefully pull and slide the cannoli shells off of the molds. Repeat with the remaining dough circles. Let the shells set to fully cool. You can make the shells in the morning and let them hang out all day until you're ready to fill them.

When ready to serve, pipe the filling into each end of the cannoli shell, slightly overfilling and swirling as you reach the ends, so it holds its shape in the cannoli. The consistency of the filling should hold on its own. Place the cannoli on a large serving platter and garnish with confectioners' *shugá*, because you're fancy. Serve within an hour so the shells don't get soggy.

CHEFIE TIPS

Make sure you chop the chocolate chips, otherwise they won't fit though the tip of the pipping bag.

Cannoli dough is firmer than pasta dough, so flatten it using your hands before feeding it through the pasta rollers to help it along. Never jam it through or it'll break the rollers.

THE BASICS

Start here to build great food.

JAR CANNING ROMA TOMATOES

Everyone does this process different, here's Momma T's way (my dear friend Chantal's Italian momma). Now you'll have fresh tomatoes at the ready for the absolute best, simple marinara (Chefie Tip on page 10) all year long to make Eggplant Rollatini (page 21), pizza sauce for Grilled Sausage and Pepperoni Pizza (page 43), or use them to make Weeknight Chili (page 67), don't add the basil, Garganelli all'Arrabbiata (page 10), Lobster Fra Diavolo Fettuccine (page 15), Short Rib Ragù Lasagna from Scratch (page 13) or Tomato Basil Soup with Grilled Cheese Croutons (page 113). For recipes that you're making that don't require basil, skip a few jars to set aside for them.

MAKES 12 (32-OUNCE [946-ML]) MASON JARS (ABOUT 2 POUNDS [908 G] PREPARED TOMATOES PLUS THEIR JUICES PER JAR)

24 pounds (11 kg) ripe Roma or plum tomatoes

kosher salt

fresh basil leaves

In a 6- or 8-quart (5.5- to 7.5-L) pot, bring water to a rolling bubble over high heat. Core the tomatoes and toss the cores into a food mill fitted with the fine disk over a large bowl. Working in batches, blanch the tomatoes in the boiling water until the skin cracks, 30 seconds to 1½ minutes.

Using a spider (handheld strainer), transfer the tomatoes to a large bowl. Once cool enough to handle, trim away any blemishes, if any. Peel away the skin and toss the skins into the food mill with the cores. Halve or quarter the tomatoes and remove the pulp and seeds, the best you can. If some seeds remain, *donta* you worry. Toss the seeds and pulp into the food mill with the skins and cores.

Rapidly turn the handle clockwise on the food mill, running the skins, cores and pulp through to release their juices. From time to time, stop and turn counterclockwise to clean the blade. Repeat until the skins, cores and pulp are fully pressed through. Discard the skins, cores and seeds.

Add the tomato puree to the tomatoes. Season lightly with salt.

Place several basil leaves into the bottom of 12 (32-ounce [946-ml]) sterilized Mason jars. Fill the jars with the tomatoes and some of the puree, filling beneath the ring (28 to 30 ounces [828 to 887 ml]). Wipe the rims and tops clean.

(continued)

JAR CANNING ROMA TOMATOES *(continued)*

In a separate medium pot, bring water to a bubble over high heat. Add the jar sealer collars and brand new lids into the water and boil, 3 to 4 minutes. Carefully remove, dry well and immediately place them onto the jars. Twist the collar ring until firmly fitted. The heat will immediately help the tacky rim stick and seal to the lid. Don't skip this step!

Place the canning rack in the bottom of a 20-quart (19-L) heavy-bottomed pot. The rack prevents the jars from banging into each other and also elevates them from the bottom of the hot pot. Add the jars, working in batches. Fill the pot with enough water to just cover the top of the jars, any higher and it could boil over. If you're using a taller pot, you can add more water. Cover the pot and bring the water to a rapid boil over high heat. Reduce the heat to medium and continue to boil, covered, 30 to 35 minutes. The water should have a steady rolling bubble, boiling over top of the lids. You want that.

Carefully remove the jars and keep them upright. As the jars are cooling for several hours, you'll hear the lid sealers pop. You want that!

Place the jars on their side on a towel to fully cool. Momma T says, "It prevents the tomatoes and their juices from separating." Cover the jars with another towel or blanket to insulate them as they are slowing cooling down. After 1 to 2 days, turn the jars right side up. Carefully remove the rings only and place on your shelf in your cabinet or pantry.

The jar canned tomatoes are good for up to 1½ years.

BRIOCHE BURGER BUNS

Stop! Make these buns. Pillowy, tender and delicious. I'm obsessed!

MAKES 10 BUNS

10 grams active dry yeast

¼ cup (48 g) granulated sugar - divided

1 cup (240 ml) warm water (105 to 110°F [40 to 43°C])

2 large eggs - divided

1 large egg yolk

3½ cups (487 g) unbleached all-purpose flour + extra for dusting

2 teaspoons (6 g) kosher salt

¼ cup (57 g) European-style unsalted butter - cut into small cubes and softened at room temperature

neutral oil (avocado or canola oil)

sesame seeds - to garnish (optional)

In a medium bowl, stir the yeast, 2 tablespoons (24 g) *shugá* and warm water. Let the mixture set until it becomes very foamy, 10 to 15 minutes.

In a small bowl, whisk 1 egg and the egg yolk together until combined.

In the bowl of a stand mixer add the flour, salt and remaining 2 tablespoons (24 g) *shugá* and use the dough hook attachment to stir together by hand. Fit the dough hook onto the stand mixer. With the mixer on low speed, pour in the egg and yeast mixture. Push the mixture down along the perimeter with a rubber spatula, coaxing the flour to pull together in a loose ball.

Once it begins to form, add the butter cubes, one at a time while mixing. Continue kneading the dough over low speed, about 10 minutes. When all the dough accumulates on the dough hook, stop the mixer and push the dough down into the bowl and continue mixing. You'll need to do this several times. The dough is going to be very sticky, *donta* you worry.

Lightly oil the inside of a large bowl and oil a piece of plastic wrap large enough to cover the bowl.

Dust a rubber spatula and your hands with flour, to help you remove the dough from the mixing bowl and transfer it to the oiled bowl. Flip and coat the dough in the oil all over and cover the bowl with the plastic wrap, oiled side down. Place the bowl in a cold oven and turn on the light. This gives the oven some heat to proof. Or, if you have the proofing function on your oven, turn it on to 100°F (37°C). Let the dough proof until doubled in size, 1 to 1½ hours.

(continued)

BRIOCHE BURGER BUNS *(continued)*

Remove the bowl and punch down the dough.

Transfer the dough to a non-floured work surface; you'll need the countertop to slightly grip the dough to roll each piece into a ball. Dust a rubber spatula and your hands with flour. Divide the dough into 10 equal pieces. Shape each piece into a ball, tucking the edges underneath and place them seam side down onto the non-floured countertop, cup it with the palm of your hand and rapidly move it in a circular motion, forming a ball. Gently flatten into 2½- to 2¾-inch- (6- to 7-cm-) diameter slightly flattened balls. Arrange 1 inch (2.5 cm) apart among a parchment paper–lined rimmed baking sheet. Cover with a clean kitchen towel. Place the baking sheet into the cold oven and turn on the light or set the proofing function to 100°F (37°C). Let the dough proof again until doubled in size, 45 minutes to 1 hour.

Remove the dough before heating the oven.

Heat the oven to 375°F (190°C).

In a small bowl, crack the remaining egg and whisk until beaten. Gently (careful not to deflate the dough) brush the tops and sides of the buns with the remaining beaten egg. Sprinkle the tops with sesame seeds, if using.

Bake until lightly golden, 12 to 14 minutes. Remove the buns to cool. Slice in half, crosswise when ready to serve.

CHEFIE TIP

Freeze any leftover buns in large zipper bags. Thaw the buns at room temperature, 30 minutes to several hours ahead in the zipper bag before serving.

OLD SCHOOL WHITE SANDWICH BREAD

Want the ultimate PB&J, grilled cheese or patty melt (page 45), or simply love bread as much as I do slathered with buttah? This is it, old-school style.

MAKES 1 LOAF

10 grams active dry yeast

1 tablespoon + 2 teaspoons (25 g) granulated sugar - divided

¾ cup (180 ml) warm water (105 to 110°F [40 to 43°C])

½ cup (120 ml) whole milk

3 tablespoons (42 g) unsalted butter - melted and cooled

3¾ cups (475 g) unbleached bread flour

2 teaspoons (12 g) kosher salt

neutral oil (canola or avocado oil)

In a medium pitcher, stir the yeast, 2 teaspoons (10 g) *shugá* and warm water. Let the mixture set until it becomes very foamy, 10 to 15 minutes. Stir the milk into the cooled melted butter. Make sure the temperature is not too hot, room temperature is ideal for the milk. We don't want to run the risk of killing the yeast when they come in contact.

In the bowl of a stand mixer, stir the flour, salt and remaining 1 tablespoon (15 g) *shugá* together by hand using the dough hook attachment, then fit the mixer with the dough hook. While the mixer is running on low speed, slowly pour in the melted butter and milk mixture, then pour in the yeast mixture and mix until combined. Push the mixture down along the perimeter with a rubber spatula, coaxing the flour to form a ball. If the dough is a tad wet after it's been mixing a minute or two, lightly dust with a little flour. If it's too dry, add a few splashes of warm water until it becomes a loose ball with a few crumbles in the bottom of the bowl but doesn't cling to the sides of the bowl. Once it forms a ball, knead over low speed until smooth, 3 to 4 minutes.

Lightly oil a medium bowl and transfer the dough to the bowl. Flip and thinly coat the dough in the oil all over. Cover with plastic wrap. Place the bowl in a cold oven and turn on the light. This gives the oven some heat to proof. If you have the proofing function on your oven, turn it on 100°F (37°C). Let set to proof until doubled in size, 1 to 1½ hours. I've found in the summer, I only need 1 hour, but in the winter, I need more like 1½ hours.

Using your hands and fingers, stretch out the dough into an 8 x 11–inch (20 x 28–cm) rectangle. Starting at the shorter side, firmly roll up the dough, like a puffy log and place it seam side down into a greased 9 x 5–inch (23 x 13–cm) loaf pan and loosely cover with a clean kitchen towel.

Return the loaf pan to the cold oven and turn on the light or set the proofing function to 100°F (37°C). Let it rise again until the dough

just clears the edge of the pan, 35 to 45 minutes. Remove the pan from the oven. Heat the oven to 350°F (177°C). Place the pan into the oven and bake until lightly golden, 30 to 35 minutes. Transfer the bread to a wire cooling rack once it's easy to handle. Cool and slice as you need into ⅜-inch- to ½-inch- (1- to 1.5-cm-) thick slices.

PEASANT BREAD

Quick, easy, delicious. You can make bread! Don't think about it, just do it!

MAKES 1 LOAF

3½ cups (468 g) unbleached all-purpose flour + more for dusting

1 (7-g [¼-oz]) packet instant dry yeast

2 teaspoons (7 g) granulated sugar

2 teaspoons (6 g) kosher salt

1 cup (240 ml) warm water (105 to 110°F [40 to 43°C]) + more as needed

2 tablespoons (30 ml) olive oil

In the bowl of a stand mixer, add the flour. Make a shallow well in the center of the flour. Add the yeast and sugar into the well. Evenly sprinkle the salt around the perimeter, not touching the yeast. Fit the mixer with the dough hook.

In a medium pitcher, add the warm water and oil and pour some of the water mixture into the well with the yeast, creating a small puddle. Let sit, 5 minutes.

With the mixer on low speed, slowly pour in the remaining water mixture. Using a rubber spatula, push down the flour around the perimeter, coaxing the flour to combine and moisten. Add a few splashes of warm water, if needed. Once the dough begins pulling together, continue kneading it on low speed, 2 to 3 minutes. The dough may slightly stick to the sides, that's okay. Remove and cover the bowl with plastic wrap. Set the bowl in an area of the house that's about 70 to 72°F (21 to 22°C). Do not place the bowl on cold stone countertops. Let the dough proof until doubled in size, 1 to 1½ hours.

Heat the oven to 400°F (204°C). Place an empty 4-quart (3.5-L) Dutch oven with the lid on in the heated oven for 30 minutes. Lightly dust your work surface with flour and transfer the dough to the floured surface. Pull each side of the dough up and fold it inward on all four sides. Flip the dough seam side down. Lightly dust the mixing bowl with flour and place the dough back into the mixing bowl and cover the bowl with plastic wrap or a towel. Let the dough rise again, 30 minutes.

Dust your fingers with flour and carefully, to avoid deflating the dough, scoop your fingers under the dough to lift it up and out. Transfer it right side up into the heated Dutch oven. Make a long slit on top of the dough with a sharp knife and lightly dust the top with flour. Cover with the lid and bake for 30 minutes. Remove the lid and continue baking until golden brown and crispy, 5 to 10 minutes. Transfer the bread to cool on a wire cooling rack. Once cooled, cover the bread with a clean kitchen towel. Serve that day.

EASY PIZZA DOUGH

There is nothing better than pizza and red wine. Now you can make your very own pizza pie from scratch. It's not hard. This dough is also great to make strombolis, calzones and panzerotti too. Saluti.

MAKES 2 PIZZA DOUGH BALLS; SERVES 6 TO 8

1 (7-g [¼-oz]) packet active dry yeast

1 teaspoon granulated sugar

¼ cup (60 ml) warm water (105 to 110°F [40 to 43°C])

3¼ cups (442 g) unbleached all-purpose flour + more for dusting

2 teaspoons (6 g) kosher salt

1 cup (240 ml) room-temperature water (about 70°F [21°C])

3 tablespoons (45 ml) olive oil + more for oiling

CHEFIE TIP

Cover the dough in a large zipper bag and refrigerate overnight or freeze, up to 2 months. Thaw or remove to room temperature, 30 minutes before preparing.

In a medium pitcher, stir the yeast, *shugá* and warm water, and let set to bloom the yeast until the mixture becomes very foamy, 10 to 15 minutes.

In the bowl of a stand mixer fitted with the dough hook, stir the flour and salt together. Add the room temperature water and 3 tablespoons (45 ml) olive oil to the pitcher with the bloomed yeast mixture and stir.

With the mixer on low speed, slowly pour in the yeast mixture until combined. Push the mixture down along the perimeter with a rubber spatula, coaxing the flour to form a ball. If the dough is a tad wet after it's been mixing a minute or two, lightly dust with a little flour; if it's too dry, add a few splashes of warm water until it becomes a loose ball with a few crumbles in the bottom of the bowl but doesn't cling to the sides of the bowl. Once it forms a ball, knead on low speed until smooth, 3 to 5 minutes. It should not stick to the sides of the bowl while mixing.

Thinly coat a large bowl with olive oil, wiping out any excess. Add the dough to the bowl, flipping to coat the dough all over. Cover the bowl with plastic wrap and place it in a cold oven and turn on the light or set the proofing function to 100°F (37°C). Let it proof until the dough doubles in size, about 1 hour. Remove the bowl from the oven and punch down the dough. Transfer the dough to a lightly floured surface and divide the dough evenly in half.

Form each dough piece into a dough ball and loosely wrap each ball in plastic wrap. The plastic wrap should cling to the dough so it doesn't form a skin but not too tight, so the dough has some room to rise. Leave the plastic-wrapped dough balls at room temperature, up to 1 hour while prepping the sauce and toppings for your pizzas or refrigerate 2 hours to overnight (see Chefie Tip). Don't leave it out at room temperature too long or it'll overproof, making it difficult to shape.

EGG YOLK PASTA DOUGH

For whatever reason, I never feel overly stuffed or uncomfortable when I eat pasta made with Italian flour and semolina. It's simply delicious, enriched with egg, tender yet chewy. You can make this dough by hand by creating a well in the middle of the flour, adding the eggs and kneading the dough, or you can let the stand mixer knead the dough for you. Both ways work great.

MAKES A LITTLE OVER 1 POUND (454 G)

5½ ounces (156 g) Tipo "00" extra-fine unbleached Italian flour + more as needed

5½ ounces (156 g) durum wheat semolina flour

½ teaspoon kosher salt + more as needed

4 large eggs yolks

1½ tablespoons (22.5 ml) olive oil

⅓ to ½ cup (80 to 120 ml) water

In the bowl of a stand mixer, stir the flour, semolina and salt to combine using the dough hook with your hand. Add the egg yolks and oil. Fit the mixer with the dough hook and turn the mixer on low speed, pushing down the flour to moisten and combine with a rubber spatula.

Slowly pour in the water, a little at a time, again pushing down the mixture with a rubber spatula to moisten and combine. When the mixture begins pulling together with a few dry crumbles in the bottom of the bowl, stop adding the water and increase the speed to medium-low, kneading the dough. After 1 to 2 minutes, the dough should form a ball, naturally pulling away from the sides of the bowl. It should not stick to the bowl. If it's sticking, lightly dust with flour. If it's too dry, add a couple splashes of water; a little goes a long way.

Continue kneading the dough until smooth, 5 to 6 minutes. Remove the dough and flatten it into a disk. Tightly wrap the dough with plastic wrap. Let it rest, 1 hour at room temperature or overnight in the refrigerator. Before working with the dough, bring the dough to room temperature, 30 minutes prior.

Using a bench scraper, divide the dough into six equal portions. Work with one piece at a time. Keep the remaining dough tightly covered in the plastic wrap while you work.

Lightly dust flour onto your work surface. Flatten the piece of dough and feed it through the feed of your pasta roller (see the Chefie Cheat Sheet on page 156).

(continued)

EGG YOLK PASTA DOUGH *(continued)*

When finished rolling out the dough, trim the edges with a pizza cutter so they're clean, not frayed. Lay the pasta sheet on a lightly floured piece of wax or parchment paper. While working with the remaining dough, cover with a clean kitchen towel. Do not stack the pasta sheets or they'll stick together.

If you're making lasagna for Short Rib Ragù Lasagna (page 13), pappardelle for Pappardelle Bolognese (page 19), garganelli for Garganelli all'Arrabbiata (page 10) or egg noodles for Classic Chicken Noodle Soup (page 118), stop right here and cut the pasta sheets as directed in my Chefie Guide below. Or change the attachment to the desired fettuccine or spaghetti cutter and feed the pasta sheets straight through, one at a time on medium speed #6 and place the pasta on a lightly floured wax or parchment paper–lined rimmed baking sheet.

Sprinkle the pasta with a little extra flour and gently toss each bundle, shaking off the excess flour, lightly coating the noodles, so they don't stick together. Form the pasta into little nests and cover with a clean kitchen towel. It's not necessary to dry out the fettuccine or spaghetti; they'll break when handling.

TO PREPARE AHEAD: You can tightly cover the kitchen towel–covered baking sheet with plastic wrap and refrigerate the pasta, up to 1 day. Or flash freeze the pasta, keeping each pasta nest separated on a sheet pan, lined with parchment paper, so they don't freeze together. Once frozen, remove each pasta nest and transfer them into large freezer zipper bags and freeze, up to 1 month. Don't stack anything on top of the bags or the pasta will break. When you're ready to cook, don't thaw the pasta, just boil an extra minute or 2.

TO COOK THE PASTA: Bring a 6-quart (5.5-L) pot of generously salted water to a rolling bubble. Plunge the pasta into the water and immediately stir so the noodles don't stick together. Cook until the pasta tightens, 2 to 3 minutes. Drain the pasta, reserving 1 cup (240 ml) of the pasta liquid, just in case you need it to thin the sauce you're using. Return the pasta to the pot, pour your desired sauce over top and stir while simmering, 1 to 2 minutes, to marry the two, absorbing the sauce into the pasta.

(continued)

EGG YOLK PASTA DOUGH *(continued)*

CHEFIE CHEAT SHEET: ROLLING OUT THE PASTA SHEETS

Speed is on #6 the entire time
#1 - 3 to 4 times, folding like a letter
#2 - 1 to 2 times, folding in half
#3 - 1 to 2 times, folding in half
#4 - 1 to 2 times, folding in half
#5 - 1 to 2 times, folding in half
#6 - 1 time, do not fold
If making pappardelle, continue to #7.

CHEFIE GUIDE: CUTTING THE PASTA SHEETS

Pappardelle (page 19): Loosely fold the pasta sheet, slightly overlapping each sheet of pasta like an accordion and cut crosswise into ¾- to ⅞-inch- (1.9- to 2.2-cm-) wide, long noodles, working with one sheet of pasta at a time. Carefully unfold, lightly dust with flour and toss. Store as directed above.

Garganelli (page 10): Using a pizza cutter, cut each pasta sheet into 2 x 2–inch (5 x 5–cm) squares. Working with one square at a time, place onto a gnocchi board (optional). Start with the point of the square and tightly roll and wrap the dough around a 5/16-inch (8-mm) wooden dowel (or a capped pen or chopstick), imprinting the grooves on the dough from the board, overlapping the points. Press the points to seal closed. Slide the tubular dough off the dowel and place on a parchment paper–lined baking sheet. Do not cover. Let the pasta dry out at room temperature so the tubes don't collapse.

Lasagna (page 13): Trim the frayed edges and cut the pasta sheets 12 inches (30.5 cm) long to comfortably fit inside a 9 x 12–inch (23 x 30.5–cm) baking dish or cut to fit the casserole dish you are using. Place the pasta sheets, side by side but not touching, on a baking sheet lined with parchment paper and tightly cover the baking sheet with a clean kitchen towel until you're ready to boil. You can refrigerate for up to 2 days. Makes 8 (12 x 6–inch [30.5 x 15–cm]) lasagna sheets.

Egg Noodles (page 118): Trim the frayed edges of each sheet of pasta. Cut down the middle of the pasta sheet lengthwise, then cut crosswise into 1-inch (2.5-cm) pieces, making 1 x 3–inch (2.5 x 7.5–cm) pieces. Loosely twist the center of the pasta pieces, creating a loose loop with flat ends. Place the pasta on a parchment paper–lined baking sheet and let the pasta dry out, flipping the pasta over halfway through drying.

UDON NOODLES FROM SCRATCH

These are so easy to make and blow away the dry, store-bought noodles. Zero comparison.

Wash your feet and slip on a clean pair of socks. The traditional way to knead udon is by foot. Yep, stomping on the dough, which is genius, since the dough is tough to roll out by hand. You'll need your body weight for kneading.

Make these noodles for my Sichuan-Style Dan Dan Noodles (page 96), my Sesame Salmon with Sweet Jalapeño Udon Noodles (in my cookbook *Cooking with Shereen from Scratch: Because You Can!*) or simply toss with my Chili Oil (page 96).

MAKES A LITTLE OVER 1 POUND (454 G); SERVES 6

2 teaspoons (6 g) kosher salt

⅔ cup (150 ml) warm water + more as needed

2¼ cups (300 g) unbleached all-purpose flour

cornstarch or potato starch - for dusting

Dissolve the salt in the ⅔ cup (150 ml) warm water.

In the bowl of a stand mixer fitted with the dough hook, add the flour. With the mixer on low speed, slowly drizzle the water into the flour, pushing the flour down using a rubber spatula to coax it together. If the dough seems dry and shaggy, add 1 tablespoon (15 ml) at a time of warm water until it becomes a loose ball with a few crumbles in the bottom of the bowl but doesn't cling to the sides of the bowl. A little water goes a long way. Be patient, give it a minute or 2 to pull together before adding another tablespoon (15 ml) water, if needed. Once it forms a ball, knead on low speed until smooth, 2 to 3 minutes.

Transfer the dough to a surface lightly dusted with cornstarch and flatten the dough with your hands. Fold the dough in half, vertically, then again horizontally and place the dough in the center of a large zipper bag, pushing out all the air.

Place the bag with the dough on the floor. Wear clean socks and knead the dough with your feet until the dough is flattened and spread out inside the bag. Don't puncture the bag. This traditional technique works like a charm since this is a very tough dough and your body weight is ideal for kneading with ease.

(continued)

UDON NOODLES FROM SCRATCH *(continued)*

Remove the dough from the bag and fold it in half vertically, then in half again horizontally and return it to the bag, again pushing out all the air. Continue kneading with your feet. Repeat this step three times total.

On the third time kneading, don't remove the dough from the bag. Leave it flattened inside the bag to rest, 2 hours at room temperature or refrigerate overnight. Remove the dough from the refrigerator 30 minutes before rolling out to remove the chill.

Divide the dough into four equal portions. Working with one at a time, lightly dust your work surface with cornstarch and roll out the dough to ³⁄₁₆-inch (5-mm) thickness. Fold the dough like an accordion, slightly overlapping and cut crosswise into ⅛- to ³⁄₁₆-inch (3- to 5-mm) wide, long noodles. Immediately toss the noodles to unravel, dusting them with cornstarch as needed to prevent sticking. Place the noodles on a parchment paper–lined baking sheet and cover them with a clean kitchen towel.

Alternatively, you can roll this out using a pasta roller: Divide the dough into four equal portions. Working with one at a time, lightly dust the dough with cornstarch to prevent sticking and pass the dough one time through the pasta roller attachment on #1, speed #6. Increase the dial to #2 thickness, speed #6, passing it through once more. Lightly dust the dough with cornstarch as needed to prevent sticking while working. Switch out the roller attachment for the fettuccine cutter attachment and pass the dough through to make noodles.

Toss the noodles lightly with cornstarch as needed to prevent sticking and place them on a parchment paper–lined baking sheet. Cover the noodles with a clean kitchen towel. Repeat with the remaining dough.

CHEFIE TIP

You can make these noodles up to 4 days ahead. Place them on a parchment paper–lined baking sheet covered with a clean kitchen towel and refrigerate. You can also freeze the noodles, up to 2 months.

QUICK MAYONNAISE FROM SCRATCH

You'll need a strong powered handheld immersion blender to whip this up. It happens quick, 30 to 40 seconds or refer to my homemade mayonnaise in my cookbook *Cooking with Shereen from Scratch: Because You Can!* (page 41) for the food processor version. No need to ever buy store-bought mayo again.

MAKES 1¼ CUPS (300 ML)

1 large egg - room temperature

1½ tablespoons (23 ml) freshly squeezed lemon juice

2 teaspoons (10 ml) white distilled vinegar

1 teaspoon Dijon mustard

½ teaspoon kosher salt

1 cup (240 ml) canola, safflower or avocado oil

In a tall glass pitcher just wide enough to fit the immersion blender, add the egg, careful not to break the yolk.

Carefully add the lemon juice, vinegar, mustard and salt, not breaking the yolk. Slowly pour in the oil. Let the mixture settle for a minute.

Insert the immersion blender, cupping the yolk over the blade. Turn the blender on high speed and don't move it for 15 to 20 seconds, while blending. Once the mayonnaise texture has formed, slowly aerate, pulling the immersion stick up and down until the mayonnaise is fully combined, 15 to 20 seconds. Taste it and season with more salt if needed.

Transfer the mayonnaise to a container with a tight-fitted lid. Refrigerate and use within 3 to 4 days.

CHEFIE TIP

Forgot to take your egg out to room temperature? Run it under lukewarm tap water to remove the chill.

HANDMADE CORN TORTILLAS (*TORTILLAS DE MAÍZ*)

If this is your first time making homemade corn tortillas, practice makes perfect. I found Goya Masarica brand gives me better success when making these corn tortillas rather than Maseca instant corn masa and hydration is key. The masa drinks it in.

MAKES 16 (5½-INCH- [14-CM-] ROUND) TORTILLAS

2 cups (240 g) instant corn masa

1 teaspoon kosher salt

1½ cups (300 ml) warm water (about 110°F [43°C]) + more as needed

In a large bowl, mix the masa and salt. Pour in the water while stirring with your hand until moistened. The mixture should not be sticky or dry; it should form into a large moistened ball.

Cover the ball with a clean, damp kitchen towel in the bowl. Let it set, 5 minutes, to fully hydrate the masa.

Heat a cast iron skillet, comal or griddle over medium-high heat, then reduce to medium to medium-low depending on which skillet you're using. It should be hot, steaming and cooking the tortillas, not burning them.

Working one at a time, use your hands to pinch a 1-ounce (35-g) piece of the masa from the ball, keeping the large ball covered with the damp towel while you work.

Dip your fingers into a bowl of warm water and rub the water over the flattened dough in the palm of your hand to moisten the masa. Fold the dough inward on all sides, then roll it into a ball. It should form a hydrated masa ball. Place the ball on a 9 x 9–inch (23 x 23–cm) piece of wax paper and top with another piece of wax paper, the same size. Alternatively, you can place the dough between two pieces of plastic cut from a large zipper bag. Press (do not squeeze) the dough using a tortilla press or a heavy-bottomed pot to flatten it into a 5½-inch (14-cm) circle.

(continued)

HANDMADE CORN TORTILLAS (*TORTILLAS DE MAÍZ*) *(continued)*

Place the tortilla on the heated skillet, comal or griddle and cook, 30 seconds to 1 minute. Flip the tortilla and cook, 30 seconds to 1 minute more, until you see a few very faint brown spots. Flip the tortilla again and press it down with your fingers or a spatula. At this point the tortilla should puff up. Once it puffs, after about 20 seconds, transfer to a clean kitchen towel and cover so it doesn't dry out. Repeat with the remaining. As each one cooks, transfer them to the kitchen towel and stack them on top of each other, keeping them covered. If the tortilla doesn't puff, *donta* you worry, they'll still be delicious.

Let the towel-covered tortillas rest, 20 minutes, to further steam, cooking the tortillas. They'll be flexible.

When you're ready to serve: reheat in the skillet, grill, griddle or comal over medium-low heat to warm and toast them, 15 to 20 seconds on each side before filling. You can store the tortillas in a large zipper bag and refrigerate, up to 1 week.

CHEFIE TIP

Make sure you dip your fingers in warm water and rub the center of the balls before rolling and pressing. It'll create steam, helping them to puff when cooking.

HOUSE-MADE FLOUR TORTILLAS (*TORTILLAS DE HARINA*)

Fluffy, tender and delicious. These are traditionally made with manteca (lard) and worked into the flour with your hands. Alternatively, you can melt the manteca and add it into water. It's not traditional but works great for ease.

MAKES 8 (8- TO 9-INCH [20- TO 23-CM]) OR 10 (6- TO 7-INCH [15- TO 18-CM]) TORTILLAS

2⅔ cups (357 g) unbleached all-purpose flour + more as needed

1½ teaspoons (9 g) kosher salt

3 tablespoons (45 ml) manteca (lard), canola or avocado oil

6½ ounces (190 ml) warm water (105 to 110°F [40 to 43°C])

In the large bowl of a stand mixer, add the flour and salt and stir it together using the dough hook by hand. If using manteca (lard), work it into the flour mixture, rubbing it between your hands until you have small pea-sized crumbles.

Fit the stand mixer with the dough hook. Turn the mixer on low and if using oil, slowly pour in the oil and water, pushing down the flour until it is evenly moistened. It may seem crumbly at this point. Be patient, it will come together when kneading. If you are using the lard, just pour in the water following the instructions.

Add a splash of warm water, if needed to pull the dough together. Increase the speed to medium and knead the dough until smooth, about 2 minutes. The dough should be supple and smooth yet slightly tacky. If it's too firm, it needs more water. Alternatively, you can mix it in a bowl and knead it by hand.

Divide the dough into 8 or 10 pieces, depending on the size tortilla you want (see above) and form it into dough balls. Immediately cover the dough balls with a clean, slightly damp kitchen towel so they don't form a skin. Let them rest, 15 minutes.

Heat a 10-inch (25-cm) cast-iron skillet over medium heat.

(continued)

HOUSE-MADE FLOUR TORTILLAS (*TORTILLAS DE HARINA*) *(continued)*

Working one at a time, lightly dust your surface and the dough ball with flour. Flatten the dough into a disk with your fingertips. If making 8 tortillas, roll each dough ball out into an 8- to 9-inch (20- to 23-cm) circle. If making 10 tortillas, roll each dough ball out into a 6- to 7-inch (15- to 18-cm) circle.

Add one tortilla at a time to the skillet, maintaining the heat between medium and medium-low. Don't burn 'em! Cook the tortillas until a couple air bubbles appear on the surface with a couple charred spots on the bottom, 30 to 45 seconds. Flip the tortillas and cook the other side, 30 to 45 seconds more. The entire tortilla may puff. *Donta* you worry, that's a good sign.

Transfer the tortillas to a clean kitchen towel and cover so they don't dry out. Repeat with the remaining dough. As each one cooks, transfer them to the kitchen towel and stack them on top of each other, keeping them covered. The steam will continue to cook them.

Once they're all cooked, transfer them to a large zipper bag and zip closed. Refrigerate, up to 1 week. As you need them, reheat the tortillas on an open flame, in the oven, on the grill or in a skillet until warmed through and pliable or fill and make my Pan-Fried Chicken Quesadillas (page 82).

HOMEMADE CHICKEN STOCK (TWO WAYS)

Anytime you roast a whole chicken, save the carcass. It makes delicious stock. Toss the carcass in a large zipper bag and refrigerate for up to 2 days or freeze up to 2 months, until you're ready to make stock. The stock will be beautifully golden. No need to add the onion skins. I've found it tints the color orangey-yellow.

MAKES ABOUT 3 QUARTS (2.8 L)

1 whole roasted chicken carcass

4 to 5 celery stalks – roughly chopped

4 carrots – tops trimmed, unpeeled and roughly chopped

1 extra large onion – peeled and chopped

4 to 5 fresh or 2 dry bay leaves

1 small bunch fresh thyme sprigs

1 small bunch fresh Italian parsley with stems

½ tablespoon black peppercorns

2 teaspoons to 1 tablespoon (12 to 15 g) kosher salt

ON THE STOVETOP

In an 8-quart (7.5-L) stock pot, add the chicken carcass, celery, carrots, onions, bay leaves, thyme, parsley and peppercorns. Pour 14 to 16 cups (3.3 L to 3.8 L) cold water into the pot and bring to a rapid bubble over high heat. Reduce the heat and simmer, covered for 4 hours. Skim and remove the foam as it rises to the surface of the stock, as needed.

Remove the pot from the heat to cool slightly. Strain the stock into a cheesecloth-lined colander set over a large heat-safe bowl. Push down on the solids, then discard. Stir in the salt. Cool completely before storing.

IN A PRESSURE COOKER

In a 6- or 8-quart (5.5- to 7.5-L) pressure cooker, add the insert pot and then add the chicken carcass, celery, carrots, onions, bay leaves, thyme, parsley and peppercorns. Pour cold water into the pot to fill to the ⅔ line, marked inside the pot. Important: Do not exceed the ⅔ line inside the pot.

Pressure cook on HIGH for 1½ hours. Use the natural release.

Remove the stock to cool slightly. Strain into a cheesecloth-lined colander set over a large heat-safe bowl. Push down on the solids, then discard. Stir in the salt. Cool completely before storing.

To store: Refrigerate the stock in clear, quart-sized containers with tight-fitting lids for several hours to overnight. Skim and remove any fat congealed on the top.

Refrigerate for several days or freeze for a few months.

HOMEMADE BEEF STOCK (TWO WAYS)

Store-bought beef stock is gross! It can't compete with making your own. I like to add a little salt to my stock for two reasons: One, it wakes up the flavor and if you've only had store-bought, tasting this enhanced version will help you realize the little effort it takes to make it is totally worth it. And two, now it's ready for soups, stews, sauces, even braises with room to spare to season to taste at the end, as desired.

I love celery leaves, so I save mine for salads or you can toss them in the stock if you like.

MAKES 2 TO 2½ QUARTS (1.9 TO 2.4 L)

4½ pounds (2 kg) beef neck and marrow bones

¼ cup (60 ml) tomato paste

avocado oil

4 to 5 celery stalks - trimmed, roughly chopped

4 large carrots - tops trimmed, unpeeled, roughly chopped

1 extra large Spanish onion - peeled, roughly chopped

1 bunch fresh thyme

1 small bunch fresh Italian parsley with stems

4 to 5 fresh or 2 dried bay leaves

½ tablespoons (3.5 g) black peppercorns

2 teaspoons (12 g) kosher salt

Heat the oven to 375°F (190°C).

On a rimmed baking sheet, place the beef bones and smear the tomato paste over the meat and bones. Don't let the tomato paste touch the sheet pan or it can burn. Rub a little avocado oil over the tomato paste, to prevent burning. Roast the bones and caramelize the tomato paste, 40 to 45 minutes. Remove and deglaze the sheet pan, if needed.

ON THE STOVETOP

In an 8-quart (7.5-L) stock pot, add the roasted bones to the pot. Deglaze the baking sheet with a little water (only if there's no burnt pieces) and add the liquid to the pot. Add the celery, carrots, onions, thyme, parsley, bay leaves and peppercorns. Pour 14 to 16 cups (3.3 L to 3.8 L) cold water into the pot and bring to a rapid bubble over high heat. Reduce the heat and simmer, covered, for 4 hours. Skim and remove any foam as it rises to the surface, as needed.

Remove the pot from the heat to cool slightly. Strain the stock into a cheesecloth-lined colander set over a large heat-safe bowl. Push down on the solids, then discard. Stir in the salt. Cool the stock completely before storing.

(continued)

HOMEMADE BEEF STOCK (TWO WAYS)

(continued)

IN A PRESSURE COOKER

In a 6- or 8-quart (5.5- to 7.5-L) pressure cooker, add the insert pot and then add the roasted bones. Deglaze the baking sheet with a little water (only if there's no burnt pieces) and add the liquid to the pot. Add the celery, carrots, onions, thyme, parsley, bay leaves and peppercorns. Pour cold water into the pot to fill to the ⅔ line, marked inside the pot. Important: Do not exceed the ⅔ line inside the pot. Pressure cook on HIGH for 1½ hours. Let it natural release, 30 minutes, then quick release.

Remove to cool slightly. Strain the stock into a cheesecloth-lined colander set over a large heat-safe bowl. Push down on the solids, then discard. Stir in the salt. Cool the stock completely before storing.

To store: Refrigerate the stock in clear, quart-sized containers with tight-fitting lids for several hours to overnight. Skim and remove any fat congealed on the top. Refrigerate the stock up to several days or freeze up to a few months.

ACKNOWLEDGMENTS

I create, develop and test all of my own recipes and film and edit my videos for my social platforms. Yes, I'm a one-man band. But, compiling this book takes a team. Sixty recipes in five (twelve- to fourteen-hour) days was a feat I could not have done alone.

Ken Goodman, I appreciate your complete dedication and commitment to long hours on set while we crafted magical photos. Thank you for your talent and capturing delicious shots.

Katie Stilo, working with you again was inspiring and fed my creativity. Thank you for expertly food styling beautiful food with me.

Dawn, a life-saver! You rock, thank you for showing up when we needed you most. I'm so grateful for you.

My girlfriends Barbie and Dionne, I loved the fact you wanted to be fed rockstar dinners every night of the shoot and while recipe testing. I'm so glad I could pamper you as you both have pampered me through our friendship.

Jeannette, thank you for recipe testing and pre-prepping to help make shoot week more organized. I'm truly grateful for all your help.

Thank you Marissa Giambelluca, Meg Baskis and the entire team at Page Street Publishing for helping me create a beautiful book. Again.

My husband, Andreas, and children, Costas and Isabella. Thank you for all your support, encouragement and patience as I work long hours pursuing my dreams. I love you more than you'll ever know. You're my life. My heart. And the best foodies I know.

ABOUT THE AUTHOR

SHEREEN PAVLIDES is a social media video creator and chef influencer reaching millions worldwide. She is an honors graduate of the Institute of Culinary Education NYC and has worked as a food stylist and on-air product host for QVC. She is also the author of the bestselling book *Cooking with Shereen from Scratch: Because You Can!* Follow her on Instagram, TikTok, Facebook and YouTube @CookingwithShereen.

INDEX